OCCASIONAL PAPER 252

Y0-EIB-977

Growth in the Central and Eastern European Countries of the European Union

Susan Schadler, Ashoka Mody, Abdul Abiad, and Daniel Leigh

INTERNATIONAL MONETARY FUND
Washington DC
2006

© 2006 International Monetary Fund

Production: IMF Multimedia Services Division
Typesetting: Alicia Etchebarne-Bourdin
Figures: Bob Lunsford

Cataloging-in-Publication Data

Growth in the Central and Eastern European countries of the European
Union/Susan Schadler . . . [et al.]—Washington, D.C.: International Monetary Fund, 2006.

      p.   cm.—(Occasional papers; 252)

    Includes bibliographical references.
    ISBN-13: 978-1-58906-554-3
    ISBN-10: 1-58906-554-9

    1. Europe, Central—Economic conditions. 2. Europe, Eastern—Economic
conditions. 3. Europe, Central—Economic policy. 4. Europe, Eastern—
Economic policy. 5. International Monetary Fund. I. Schadler, Susan.
II. International Monetary Fund. III. Series: Occasional paper (International
Monetary Fund); no. 252.

HC244.G65 2006

Price: US$30.00
(US$28.00 to full-time faculty members and
students at universities and colleges)

Please send orders to:
International Monetary Fund, Publication Services
700 19th Street, N.W., Washington, D.C. 20431, U.S.A.
Tel.: (202) 623-7430   Telefax: (202) 623-7201
E-mail: publications@imf.org
Internet: http://www.imf.org

Contents

Tables

The following conventions are used in this publication:

• In tables, a blank cell indicates "not applicable," ellipsis points (. . .) indicate "not available," and 0 or 0.0 indicates "zero" or "negligible." Minor discrepancies between sums of constituent figures and totals are due to rounding.

• An en dash (–) between years or months (for example, 2005–06 or January–June) indicates the years or months covered, including the beginning and ending years or months; a slash or virgule (/) between years or months (for example, 2005/06) indicates a fiscal or financial year, as does the abbreviation FY (for example, FY2006).

• "Billion" means a thousand million; "trillion" means a thousand billion.

• "Basis points" refer to hundredths of 1 percentage point (for example, 25 basis points are equivalent to ¼ of 1 percentage point).

As used in this publication, the term "country" does not in all cases refer to a territorial entity that is a state as understood by international law and practice. As used here, the term also covers some territorial entities that are not states but for which statistical data are maintained on a separate and independent basis.

Preface

Having smoothly acceded to the European Union (EU) in May 2004, the overarching objective for the EU's new member states is to continue raising living standards to Western European levels. This Occasional Paper examines the progress toward income convergence achieved by the the EU's eight Central and Eastern European countries thus far, the prospects for further income convergence over the medium term, and the policy challenges that these countries will face in facilitating the catch-up process.

The paper was prepared by a team led by Susan Schadler and Ashoka Mody, with Abdul Abiad and Daniel Leigh. The paper benefited from comments by various departments of the IMF; by participants at a September 2005 conference on "European Enlargement: Implications for Growth" in Washington, D.C., and at a March 2006 conference on "New Europe, New Frontiers, New Challenges, New Opportunities" in Prague; and by participants at seminar presentations in Tallinn and Warsaw and at the IMF's European Department. Material presented in this study was originally prepared as background for an IMF Executive Board seminar held in February 2006. The Acting Chair's concluding remarks are reproduced on pages 53–54 of this publication.

The authors would like to thank Indra Mahadewa, Lina Shoobridge, Sylvia Young, and Indira Bhimani for assistance in preparing the manuscript; David Velazquez-Romero for excellent research assistance; and Esha Ray of the External Relations Department for editing the manuscript and coordinating production of the publication. The opinions expressed in the paper are those of the authors and do not necessarily reflect the views of national authorities, the IMF, or IMF Executive Directors.

Abbreviations

CE-5	Refers to Czech Republic, Hungary, Poland, Slovakia, and Slovenia
CEEC	Central and Eastern European country
EBRD	European Bank for Reconstruction and Development
EU	European Union
FDI	Foreign direct investment
GDP	Gross domestic product
GFS	*Government Finance Statistics*
ICRG	*International Country Risk Guide*
ICT	Information and communication technology
OECD	Organization for Economic Cooperation and Development
PPP	Purchasing power parity
PWT	Penn World Tables
TFP	Total factor productivity
WDI	*World Development Indicators*
WEO	*World Economic Outlook*

I Overview

The paramount economic objective of the Central and Eastern European countries (CEECs) is to raise living standards to Western European levels.[1] After a half century of largely misdirected development, the task is formidable and will require concerted macroeconomic and structural policies focused on achieving strong growth with due regard for vulnerabilities inherent in any rapid catch-up. In many respects, this process resembles that in other regions, and the CEECs will be well advised to draw lessons from experiences elsewhere. But, in other respects—particularly the advantages of membership in the European Union (EU)—the CEECs have unique opportunities from trade-induced competition, pressures for policy reform, and greater financial integration.

The strength of the growth record in the CEECs since the end of central planning is open to interpretation. From a 15-year perspective—that is, including the initial transition shock—the record is no better than average by the standards of emerging market countries. In the past decade, however, growth in most of the CEECs has been clearly above the average of emerging market countries; in fact, the three Baltic countries (Estonia, Latvia, and Lithuania) have been in the top five emerging market performers. Evaluating the performance of the CEECs is complicated by three developments that are difficult to disentangle: a recovery from the immediate post-central-planning drop in output; the emergence of policies and institutional conditions (including EU membership) that enhanced catch-up potential; and global economic developments favorable to investment and growth in emerging market countries. Thus, determining whether the strength of the past decade has been more a bounce back from the initial posttransition setbacks in a period relatively favorable for emerging market countries or more the result of conditions that will support continuing growth requires an examination of the underlying influences.

In several respects, the CEECs' growth experience during the past decade was unusual by emerging market country standards.

- *Massive labor shedding occurred* alongside relatively rapid output growth. Employment rates dropped from among the highest in emerging market countries at the end of central planning to well below average.

- *Relatively low domestic savings rates were supplemented by foreign savings*, particularly in the three Baltic countries.

- *Nevertheless, capital accumulation made modest contributions to growth*—on average smaller than in the most dynamic Asian countries, though larger than in Latin America.

- *Growth was dominated by remarkable increases in total factor productivity (TFP)*. TFP growth was almost double that in other emerging market country groups. This is not surprising in view of the inefficiencies inherited from central planning, which left much scope for managerial improvements, labor shedding, and gains from interindustry resource reallocation.

- *The recent record, however, suggests the possibility of a two-speed catch-up:* growth in the three Baltic countries having pulled substantially ahead of that in the five Central European countries (the Czech Republic, Hungary, Poland, Slovakia, and Slovenia; henceforth, CE-5).

Looking ahead, the critical question is whether TFP growth can be sustained, and, if not, what would replace it as the underpinning of a rapid catch-up. Differing time lines of transition may shed light on this question. On average, countries that recovered earliest from the transition shock—broadly the CE-5, but especially Poland and Slovenia—have seen a substantial diminution in TFP growth (though it remains higher than in other emerging market country groups). This is broadly reflected in lower output growth, although a halt or slowing in labor shedding has been a mitigating influence. In contrast, TFP growth in the later-to-recover Baltics has continued to rise. Assuming that the slowdown in TFP continues in the CE-5 and spreads to the Baltic countries, other sources of growth will be essential to sustain a rapid catch-up. Greater labor use is an obvious candidate: to live up to its growth poten-

---

[1]The CEECs comprise the Czech Republic, Estonia, Hungary, Latvia, Lithuania, Poland, the Slovak Republic (henceforth, Slovakia), and Slovenia.

tial, every country—particularly Poland, Hungary, and Slovakia—must decisively turn around its labor market performance. Also, investment rates will need to rise. Finally, financing will be the major challenge in these generally low-saving countries.

Whatever the source of growth, prospects will depend on how well countries do in establishing macroeconomic and structural conditions conducive to sustained growth. Building on global studies of links between growth and a variety of environmental and policy characteristics, some broad conclusions emerge on the conditions for a rapid catch-up. Robust linkages come from certain environmental features (such as initial income gaps, population growth, and historical trade relationships), as well as conditions more subject to policy influence (such as the quality of legal and economic institutions, size of government, real cost of investment, educational attainment, openness to trade, and inflation). In general, the CEECs do reasonably well in meeting these conditions (relative, for example, to an East Asian sample[2]). On average, however, the differences tend to favor growth in the Baltic countries over the CE-5, reinforcing other indications that a two-speed catch-up may be emerging. Some broad conclusions stand out.

- Initial income gaps vis-à-vis advanced economies—reflecting catch-up potentials—were generally smaller in the CEECs than in East Asia, though in three countries (Poland, Latvia, and Lithuania) the gaps were larger than the East Asian average even as of 2004.

- Slow population growth has favored catch-up in the CEECs (especially the Baltics) over East Asia, although, over time, aging could shift this advantage.

- The Baltics and East Asia have benefited decisively relative to the CE-5 from faster growth in their historical export markets—Baltic exports are more oriented toward the Nordic countries and Russia and CE-5 exports more toward Germany and its immediate neighbors.

- The CE-5 have had the edge on institutional development (regulatory frameworks and governance) relative to East Asia and even the Baltics, though the latter have been catching up rapidly.

- On other policy variables, the CEECs have had differing strengths, which taken together have had roughly comparable effects on growth. All countries are highly open to trade. East Asian countries on average have smaller governments, although the

Baltics come a close second. Years of schooling are highest on average in East Asia, but more complex educational considerations, which are undoubtedly important, may stack up differently. Relative prices of investment goods are broadly similar.

Moreover, European integration stands to play a pivotal role in supporting a rapid catch-up in the CEECs. At one level, of course, are the opportunities offered by substantial EU transfers—likely to be some 2–3 percent of GDP a year for some time. Probably more important but less easy to quantify will be the benefits from closer institutional, trade, and financial integration with Western Europe. These are already evident in growing trade volumes, low risk premia, and rising use of foreign savings in the CEECs; further changes in these directions are likely, especially for countries that commit to early euro adoption. But alongside the scope for hastening the catch-up are the risks that foreign savings will finance insufficiently productive spending or that the consumption smoothing turns into excessive private or government spending.

Estimates of a simple growth and current account framework, using European data, provide some comfort in this regard. They indicate that thus far foreign savings have contributed significantly and appropriately to growth in most CEECs. Most, even with large current account deficits, have growth rates within ranges that should result (according to the experience of the countries included in the sample) from the foreign savings used. Moreover, distinctions between the effects of foreign direct investment (FDI) and non-FDI financing are not large—both have contributed significantly to growth. In other words, to the extent that integration is facilitating increased use of foreign savings even when it is not FDI, it appears to be giving CEECs a growth advantage over other emerging market countries. Variations across countries are, however, large—from Estonia, where current account deficits exceed the range indicated as consistent with recent growth rates, to Poland, where they fall short of that range.

Nevertheless, some measures of vulnerabilities, especially in the Baltic countries and Hungary, are worrisome. Various combinations of high external debt ratios, rapid credit growth (a sizable share in foreign currency), and, in the Baltics, low reserve coverage of short-term debt create a picture similar, for some countries, to that in East Asia prior to 1997. Some mitigating factors—high reserves in the CE-5, strong fiscal positions in the Baltics, relatively high standards of transparency and governance, well-supervised and predominantly foreign-owned banks—are reassuring. While a full analysis of vulnerabilities is beyond the scope of this paper, even the summary picture of vulnerability indicators points to challenges for IMF surveillance.

Rapid income convergence will be the essential context of IMF surveillance in the CEECs for the foresee-

---

[2]The East Asian economies considered are China, Hong Kong SAR, Indonesia, Korea, Malaysia, the Philippines, Singapore, Taiwan Province of China, and Thailand.

able future. Sound near-term macroeconomic policies are needed to foster a benign setting for growth. Equally important will be identifying and supporting conditions that spur growth and position countries to benefit from European integration; some of these, such as institutional development and the appropriate role of government, will be at one remove from the traditional focus of surveillance. Nevertheless, they are critical to outcomes for growth, and, all told, sustaining high growth is the ultimate economic objective for each CEEC.

Within this context, a key role for surveillance will be to keep a sharp eye on vulnerabilities. A rapid catch-up inherently involves risks, whether from the large-scale use of foreign savings, the rapid growth in financial markets and bank intermediation, or simply the rapid pace of economic change. Certainly, policies to mitigate these risks and make them more transparent are critical. In this vein, the IMF needs to press governments to establish cushions against shocks; contribute to domestic savings appropriately through sizable fiscal surpluses when catch-ups are rapid; avoid disincentives to private saving; support strong financial supervision; ensure strong cor-

porate governance and efficient bankruptcy procedures; and increase transparency across the spectrum of economic activities. The IMF also needs to be an advocate of policies that will enable the early adoption of the euro—the growth-enhancing and vulnerability-reducing opportunity unique to the CEECs.

But, fundamentally, rapid catch-up will be associated with vulnerabilities. The use of foreign savings entails exposure to foreign creditors and investors; in countries that started with minimal banking systems, rapid credit growth is almost inevitable, and where households had little or no access to credit, growing confidence in the future means sizable borrowing to smooth consumption. The macroeconomic picture of any successful CEEC will not be free from risks. The task for surveillance will be to distinguish when policies with an overarching orientation of supporting a rapid catch-up are and are not appropriate, identify policy changes that are needed, and recognize that some developments, which in more advanced or less opportunity-laden countries would indicate serious vulnerabilities, are an inescapable part of the catching-up process.

II   Scope of the Study

In the past 15 years, the IMF's dialogue with the eight new CEEC members of the EU has been about transitions.[3] The first transition was from central planning to market-oriented policies and the next from being neighbors to being members of the EU. The accomplishments have been significant: after regaining pre-transition GDP and stabilization, the countries have become attractive destinations for international capital (Figure 2.1). The efforts behind these successes gave substance first to the IMF's lending arrangements and, more recently, to surveillance.

The central challenge now—to catch up to advanced EU income levels—is matched by unique opportunities. The focus of policies is to create the basis for strong growth, while avoiding disruptive breaks in progress or conditions that would produce costly misallocations of resources. EU membership should make these efforts easier. Growing financial integration into Europe has enhanced each country's ability to draw on foreign savings; the adoption of the euro promises to eliminate currency risk premia and boost trade; and with growth-oriented policies these opportunities should hasten the catch-up.

A two-speed catch-up—rapid in the Baltics and slower in the Central European countries—is, however, emerging as a distinct possibility. Although average growth since transition is broadly similar across the eight countries, growth in the three Baltic countries has surpassed that in the CE-5 in the past five years. Of course, differences exist within these two groups—Slovakia's recent gains relative to the other CE-5 countries being an important example. But if the pattern persists, it could affect investors' actions and become self-reinforcing. The slower-growing countries will therefore need to rise to the challenge of regional competition.

The emergence of some signs of vulnerabilities is inherent in any rapid catch-up, especially one involving large-scale use of foreign savings. Although a full assessment of vulnerabilities is beyond the scope of this paper, it attempts to put these signs into perspective. The analysis points to the consonance in some countries between more rapid growth and large-scale use of foreign savings. Nevertheless, a clear challenge for surveillance will be to ensure that catch-up does not generate excessive vulnerabilities.

The paper is organized as follows. Section III records the region's growth performance, using other emerging market countries as comparators and a growth-accounting framework to identify the sources of growth. Section IV outlines two growth scenarios that illustrate the range of investment and productivity growth rates under an ambitious income catch-up objective. Section V draws on the extensive literature on empirical growth equations and uses updated cross-country growth analyses to identify strengths and weaknesses in the region. Section VI focuses on one aspect of integration with Europe: the opportunity to supplement domestic savings with foreign savings intermediated through European financial markets. Section VII concludes with implications for IMF surveillance.

---

[3]Because of the commonality of regional issues, the focus is on the Czech Republic, Estonia, Hungary, Latvia, Lithuania, Poland, Slovakia, and Slovenia.

Figure 2.1. Macroeconomic Trends in the CEECs, 1990–2004

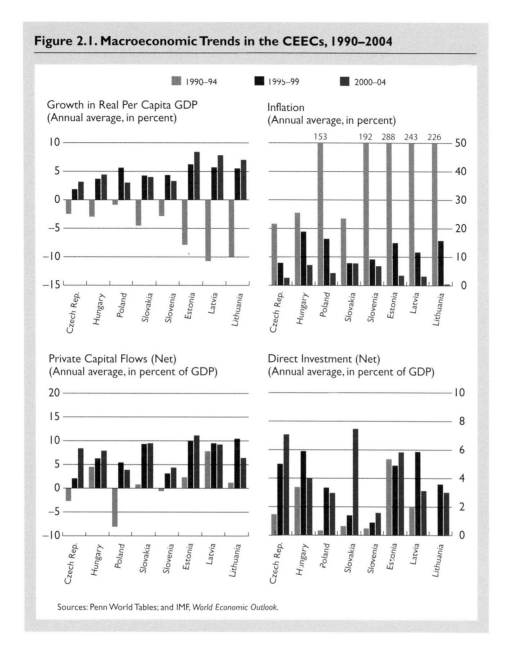

Sources: Penn World Tables; and IMF, *World Economic Outlook.*

III The Record: Enduring Strengths or a Bounce Back?

From one perspective, focusing on the past decade, growth in the CEECs has been impressive. Following sharp output losses in the initial transition period, the CEECs have been among the stronger performing emerging market countries. During 1990–94, when the costs of transition from central planning were largest, per capita GDP fell in each of the CEECs (Figure 3.1).[4] But as significant policy reforms and institutional developments paid dividends, recoveries were generally rapid (Figure 3.2).[5] Between 1995 and 1999, even with the Russian shock, all but Lithuania and the Czech Republic were squarely in the top half of emerging market growth performers. Since 2000, the Baltic countries have pulled rapidly ahead of the CE-5, placing them among the top five emerging market performers in terms of growth. Nevertheless, CE-5 growth rates were still in the top half of emerging market countries.

But the broad sweep of developments since 1990 raises a concern. From this perspective, only Poland and Estonia come out in the top half of emerging market country performers, and even they are well below the fastest-growing countries. This record then begs the question of whether the relatively strong performance since 1995 owes more to a bounce back from the sharp, early-transition losses, particularly in the Baltics, than to enduring strengths. Similarly, does the gap between recent growth in the Baltics and in the CE-5 reflect fundamental differences in policies and growth potential, or simply the reversal from their later and larger early-transition drop and sharper fallout from the Russian crisis? It will be several years before answers to these questions are clear. In the meantime, the continuation of relatively rapid recent growth cannot be treated as a given.

A distinctive characteristic of the CEECs' performance since 1995 has been small, or even negative, contributions of labor input.[6] Employment rates (persons employed as a share of working-age population) fell sharply during much of the 1990s (Figure 3.3), reflecting a variety of transition effects. State-owned enterprises were downsized or privatized; permanent unearned incomes (through preretirement benefits and disability pensions) weakened job-search incentives and discouraged retraining for the new market economy; and barriers to regional labor mobility and other labor market rigidities further contributed to long-term structural unemployment (Keane and Prasad, 2000; Estevão, 2003; Schiff and others, 2006; and Choueiri, 2005). In this respect, the CEECs stand out among emerging market countries, where labor input has typically contributed substantially to growth (Figure 3.4). Although labor use has now stabilized, employment rates are still below the average for emerging market countries, except in the Czech Republic, Estonia, and Latvia (Figure 3.5).

Capital has provided a substantial contribution to growth (see Figure 3.4). On average, the contribution of capital accumulation to growth has been lower than in East Asia or in the top emerging market country performers, but greater than in Latin America. Within the CEECs, however, the range of investment rates has been large and in some cases relationships to growth have been among emerging market outliers (Figure 3.6). At one extreme, the Czech Republic has had particularly strong investment; its relatively slow output growth suggests either low efficiency of investment and high amortization rates or long lags in the coming to fruition of investment. At the other extreme, the Baltics managed rapid growth in the past few years with moderate investment rates.

A key question is whether relatively low savings rates are holding back investment. Savings rates in the CEECs are generally low, with only the Czech Republic and Slovenia firmly in the upper half and Slovakia in the center of the emerging market

---

[4]Emerging market countries are a group of 37 middle- and low-income countries that have significant interactions with world capital markets. They comprise countries in the Morgan Stanley Capital International Emerging Markets Index, the CEECs, Bulgaria, and Romania. For the analytical usefulness of the emerging market categorization, see Rogoff and others (2004).

[5]Fischer, Sahay, and Végh (1996); Havrylyshyn and van Rooden (2000); Campos and Coricelli (2002); and EBRD (2004) establish the effect of stabilization policies and institutional development on the speed of recovery from initial output losses.

[6]This conclusion stands even when account is taken of hours worked; average weekly hours worked in the CEECs have been stable or have declined slightly in the past decade.

Figure 3.1. Emerging Market Economies: Growth in Real PPP GDP Per Capita, 1990–2004[1]

(Average annual percent change)

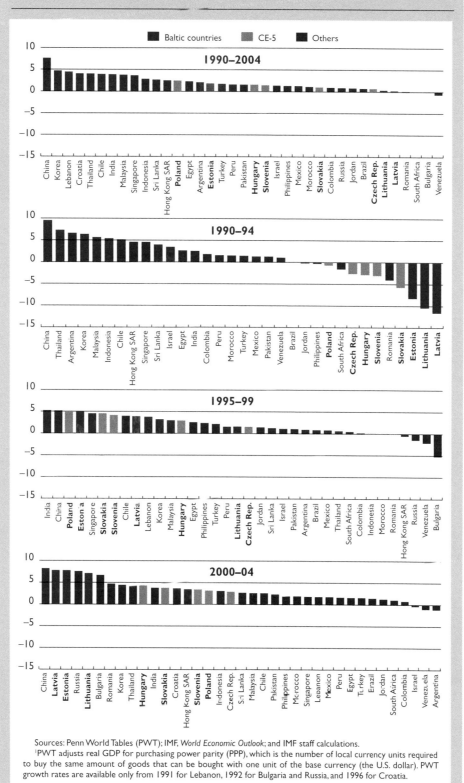

Sources: Penn World Tables (PWT); IMF, *World Economic Outlook*; and IMF staff calculations.

[1]PWT adjusts real GDP for purchasing power parity (PPP), which is the number of local currency units required to buy the same amount of goods that can be bought with one unit of the base currency (the U.S. dollar). PWT growth rates are available only from 1991 for Lebanon, 1992 for Bulgaria and Russia, and 1996 for Croatia.

Figure 3.2. CEECs and Other Emerging Market Regions: Growth in Real Per Capita GDP
(In percent)

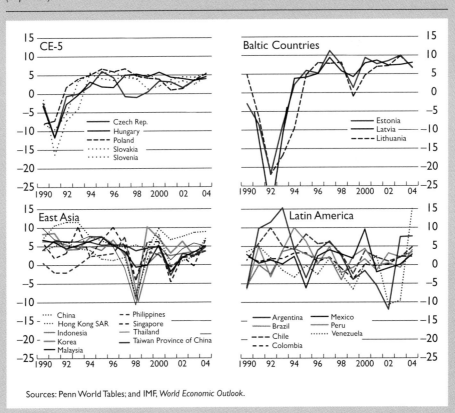

Sources: Penn World Tables; and IMF, *World Economic Outlook*.

Figure 3.3. Employment Rates in the CEECs
(In percent of population, ages 15–64)

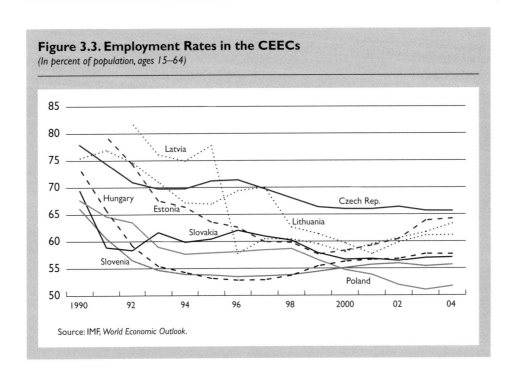

Source: IMF, *World Economic Outlook*.

Figure 3.4. Contributions to Average GDP Growth
(In percent)

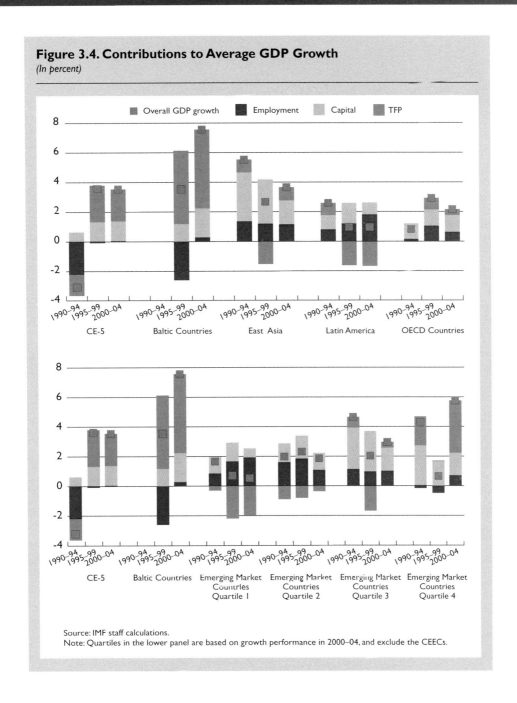

Source: IMF staff calculations.
Note: Quartiles in the lower panel are based on growth performance in 2000–04, and exclude the CEECs.

distribution (Figure 3.7). With considerably more variation in investment rates (the Czech Republic, Estonia, and Latvia at the higher end of the emerging market country spectrum and Poland at the lower end), foreign savings have played a key role in several countries.

Another distinguishing feature of CEEC growth has been an especially high contribution of TFP to growth. Measured as a residual, the size of the contribution is necessarily approximate. To the extent

that capital is underestimated (e.g., because of overestimates of depreciation) or gray market employment is hiding actual labor inputs, TFP is overestimated. Still, it is widely accepted qualitatively that productivity gains have accounted for a substantially larger share of growth in the CEECs than in other emerging market countries and that the Baltics stand out in this regard. Within-industry efficiency gains—from privatization, increased market incentives, the adoption of new technologies and managerial methods, and

Box 3.1. Compositional Shifts in Output: Implications for Productivity Growth

Caselli and Tenreyro (2005), examining broad sectoral data (agriculture, industry, and services), find that productivity gaps between CEECs and advanced economies arise mainly from lower productivity in each sector. They find that reallocation of resources to more productive sectors has helped reduce the gap, but that this has not been an important source of productivity growth. Industry- and firm-level data generally support these conclusions. Specifically, labor shares have been broadly stable across industrial sectors, suggesting that labor reallocation has not contributed to an increase in labor productivity. Indeed, labor reallocation has had small negative effects on productivity in some CEECs (see table).

Firm-level data, available at this time only for Hungary (Kátay and Wolf, 2006), however, suggest that new investment has been an instrument for resource reallocation, reflected in increased shares of the high-technology sectors in industrial production. Information and communication technology (ICT) sectors, which have relatively high total factor productivity (TFP) levels and growth rates, have also risen from less than 10 percent to more than 30 percent of industrial production in the past decade (see figure). The implication is that continued strong productivity growth will depend in part on "climbing the technology ladder" and rapid productivity growth in the ICT sectors. Given the relatively small share of ICT-producing sectors in total output in most CEECs, however, Piatkowski (2006) argues that ICT-producing sectors cannot drive the convergence process; instead, increased use of ICT by other sectors will be the important driver of productivity growth.

Labor Productivity in the CEECs, 1994–2002

	Czech Rep.	Estonia	Hungary	Lithuania	Latvia	Poland	Slovakia	Slovenia
Total labor productivity growth, 1994–2002	42.4	100.3	90.0	84.6	68.0	97.9	87.7	32.2
Within-industry gains in productivity	51.9	109.6	73.8	73.4	64.5	92.4	85.6	29.3
Of which: Gains due to reallocation of labor across sectors	−9.5	−9.2	16.2	11.2	3.5	5.5	2.1	2.9

Source: IMF staff calculations.

the bounce back from sharp output losses in the initial stages of transition—undoubtedly played a significant role in raising production levels without commensurate increases in the inputs. But shifts in the composition of output toward high-productivity sectors appear also to be playing a role (Box 3.1). Whether the TFP gains achieved thus far have eliminated the most egregious inefficiencies of central planning—and will therefore soon trail off—is a key question for prospective growth.

In sum, this review, which shows the greatest commonality across the CEECs in their low labor utilization and high TFP growth, also points to a few key questions:

• To what extent have the relatively rapid growth rates since the mid-1990s been the result of favorable

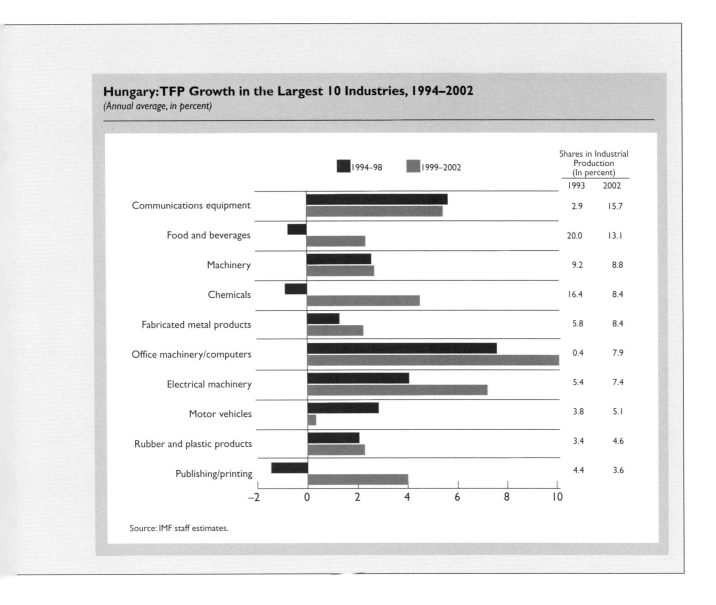

Hungary: TFP Growth in the Largest 10 Industries, 1994–2002
(Annual average, in percent)

	■ 1994–98 ■ 1999–2002	Shares in Industrial Production (In percent)	
		1993	2002
Communications equipment		2.9	15.7
Food and beverages		20.0	13.1
Machinery		9.2	8.8
Chemicals		16.4	8.4
Fabricated metal products		5.8	8.4
Office machinery/computers		0.4	7.9
Electrical machinery		5.4	7.4
Motor vehicles		3.8	5.1
Rubber and plastic products		3.4	4.6
Publishing/printing		4.4	3.6

Source: IMF staff estimates.

underlying conditions that will sustain growth, or of bounce backs from the large output losses in the early transition period?

• What are the policy priorities for sustaining high growth in the Baltics and raising them in the CE-5? What can be learned from the experience of other countries?

• Is there a problem with the recent experience, particularly in the Baltic countries, of increases in capital input financed by large capital inflows?

• To what extent does integration with Western Europe provide opportunities for growth that fundamentally differentiate the CEECs from other emerging market countries?

Figure 3.5. Employment and Activity Rates in Emerging Market Economies, 2004
(In percent of working-age population)

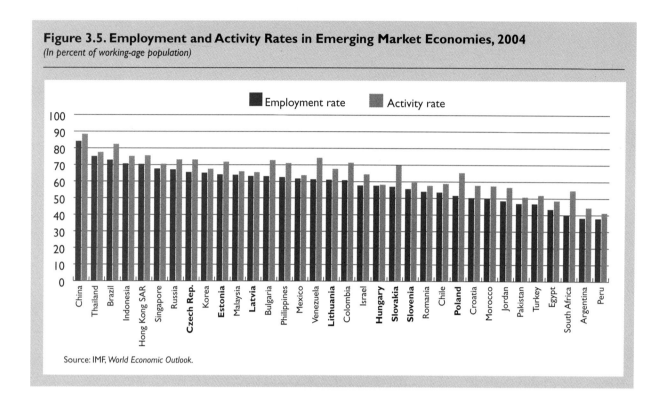

Source: IMF, *World Economic Outlook.*

Figure 3.6. Investment and Growth in Emerging Market Economies, 2000–04

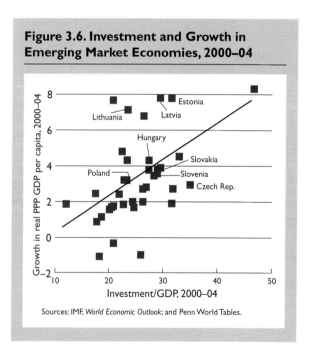

Sources: IMF, *World Economic Outlook*; and Penn World Tables.

Figure 3.7. Savings and Investment Rates in Emerging Market Economies, 2004
(In percent of GDP)

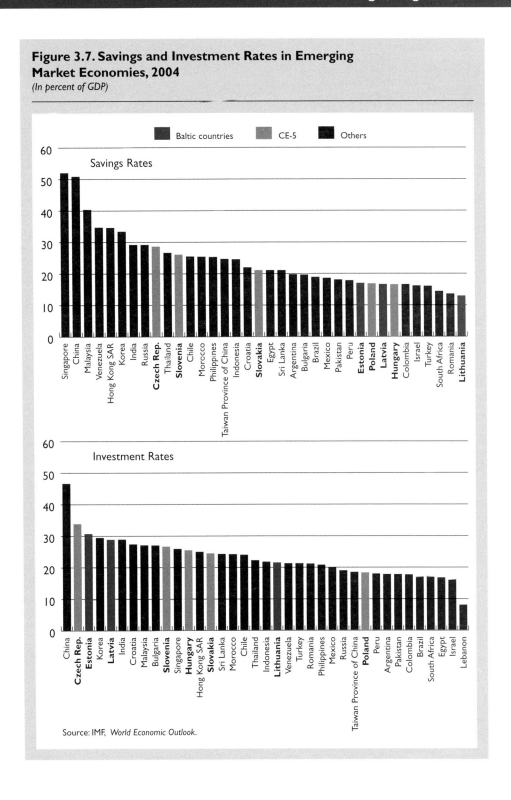

Source: IMF, *World Economic Outlook*.

IV Growth Scenarios: Possible Paths for the Catch-Up

The speed at which income gaps with the euro area could be closed varies considerably across the CEECs (Table 4.1). Countries with per capita incomes close to the euro area average need to go a shorter distance and hence are better positioned to achieve income convergence. At about $19,000 (in real purchasing power parity (PPP) terms), Slovenia's annual per capita income was 74 percent of the euro area average in 2004. At the other extreme, Latvia's per capita income of about $11,000 was 43 percent of the euro area average. If per capita incomes in the euro area grow at 2 percent a year, Slovenia, which has the shortest distance to go, can, at its current growth rate, reach 90 percent of the euro area average in 12 years. Even if growth slows, as the analysis in the next section suggests it will, 90 percent of the euro area average could be achieved in about 16 years. The relatively low-income but rapidly growing Baltics are well positioned to close half their gaps in the next 10–15 years, even if growth slows from recent rates. At the other extreme, Poland with both a relatively low per capita income and low growth could take over 70 years to reach 90 percent of the euro area average barring underlying changes to growth prospects.

Catch-up will be helped by raising employment but will depend more significantly on increased capital-labor ratios and productivity of resource use. Employment rates are low when seen in an international context. Most, however, are only modestly lower than the average in the euro area, and a few are equivalent to or even exceed the euro area average (Table 4.2). Still, countries will need to aim for higher employment rates alongside similar efforts in the euro area. From the catch-up point of view, the greatest scope for advancement lies in increasing the capital-labor ratios, which range from less than a fifth to about half of the euro area average, and are ordered precisely according to gaps in per capita GDP. High rates of investment will, therefore, be important. TFP gaps, in the range of one-third to two-thirds, are smaller than those for capital-labor ratios, but they are substantial and catch-up possibilities will depend crucially on raising productivity.

A step up in labor input will be an essential contribution to growth. If employment rates can be raised steadily by about ½ percentage point a year and popu-

lations remain stable, labor input will grow at a rate of just under 1 percent a year, contributing about ½ percentage point annually to income per capita growth. This trajectory, also envisaged in OECD (2004), would translate into a cumulative 5–6 percent increase in GDP per capita over the next 10 years. If increased participation is achieved principally by bringing low-productivity workers into the workforce, the growth dividend will be less.

Even assuming such a contribution from employment, large increases in investment and productivity would be needed for a rapid catch-up. This is illustrated by considering investment and productivity requirements needed to close half the 2004 income gap with the euro area. An ambitious policy objective would be to reduce the half-life predicted in Table 4.1 by 20 percent. For example, instead of closing half its income gap with the euro area in 20 years, the challenge to Slovakia would be to close it in 16 years. Two scenarios define the possible demands on productivity growth and investment:

- The first scenario fixes the productivity growth rate and determines the required investment rate to achieve the ambitious policy objective defined above. The long-term productivity growth is assumed to be around 1.6 percent a year, the average achieved by East Asian economies during 1990–2004. Since the Baltic countries currently exceed this productivity growth by a large margin, their rate of productivity growth is assumed to decline gradually over the next 10 years to 1.6 percent a year.

- The second scenario fixes investment/GDP at their current (2000–04) average and determines productivity growth rates needed to achieve the targeted catch-up.

In the first scenario, with productivity growth set at realistic, but high, rates, investment would need to be extremely strong in some countries (Table 4.3). The Czech Republic, Hungary, and Slovakia would need to raise investment rates by between 12 and 15 percentage points to between 35 percent and 42 percent of GDP. Others would need smaller but still significant increases. The large jumps reflect the combination of

Table 4.1. CEECs: Convergence with Euro Area Income Per Capita[1]

	2004 Income Per Capita Relative to Euro Area, PPP (In percent)	Based on Actual 2000–04 Growth		Based on Predicted 2005–09 Growth[2]	
		Years to close half the income gap	Years to reach per capita income ratio of 90 percent	Years to close half the income gap	Years to reach per capita income ratio of 90 percent
Czech Rep.	69	14	26	11	19
Estonia	49	6	16	12	34
Hungary	59	10	24	14	33
Latvia	43	7	22	14	41
Lithuania	46	7	21	12	33
Poland	46	27	79	25	73
Slovakia	52	17	45	20	54
Slovenia	74	8	12	10	16

Sources: World Bank, *World Development Indicators*; and IMF staff calculations.

[1] The convergence half-life is calculated as $\ln(2)/\beta$, where $\beta = (g - g^*)/\ln(Y/Y^*)$, g is per capita income growth, Y is the per capita income level in PPP terms, and * indicates the euro area.

[2] Predictions drawn from the empirical estimates in Section V.

Table 4.2. Decomposing the Income Gap Between the Euro Area and the CEECs

	Per Capita Income (Real PPP, U.S. dollar)	Income Ratio Versus Euro Area	Capital Per Worker		Employment Rate		Total Factor Productivity (TFP)	
			U.S. dollar per worker	Relative to euro area (In percent)	In percent	Relative to euro area (In percent)		Relative to euro area (In percent)
Czech Rep.	17,937	69	50,016	34	64.2	102	304	40
Estonia	12,773	49	32,269	22	63.0	100	321	42
Hungary	15,399	59	41,295	28	56.8	90	336	44
Latvia	11,148	43	28,329	19	62.3	99	288	38
Lithuania	12,051	46	22,008	15	61.2	97	321	42
Poland	11,921	46	31,844	22	51.7	82	367	48
Slovakia	13,437	52	38,193	26	57.0	91	277	36
Slovenia	19,251	74	64,857	44	65.3	104	490	64

Sources: World Bank, *World Development Indicators*; Eurostat; IMF, *World Economic Outlook*; and IMF staff calculations.

Note: TFP is calculated as $Y/(K^{0.35}.L^{0.65})$.

currently high productivity growth, which would fall in this scenario to 1.6 percent a year, and the fact that capital-output ratios are already relatively high (especially in the Czech Republic). While capital-labor ratios will rise as a consequence of the higher investment rates, they will still remain substantially below the euro area average. Although the investment rates implied by this scenario have been achieved in some East Asian countries, they have been supported there by significantly higher domestic savings rates than in the CEECs.

The second scenario, which fixes CEEC investment relative to GDP at the 2000–04 averages, shows a significant productivity challenge (Table 4.4). Among the CE-5, the required TFP growth rates are for the most part clustered around 3 percent—a substantial increase for the Czech Republic and Poland and at recent, relatively high rates for Hungary and Slovakia. For the Baltics, maintaining current investment rates along with an ambitious catch-up objective would be possible with productivity growth rates in the range of 3½ percent to 4½ percent a year—rates that are lower than averages for the past five years but still high by emerging market country standards. A key question for such scenarios is whether high TFP growth could occur in the absence of stronger investment.

The conditions underlying these scenarios illustrate the challenges CEECs face in sustaining a rapid catch-up. The literature has similarly emphasized the policy

Table 4.3. Scenario 1: Speeding Up Convergence in the CEECs Through Higher Investment

	Target Growth Rate (In percent a year)[1]	Contributions (in Percent) of			Investment		Total Factor Productivity (TFP) Growth
		TFP[2]	Labor[3]	Capital[4]	Required	2000–04 average	2000–04 average
Czech Rep.	4.3	1.6	0.5	2.2	42.2	27.2	1.5
Estonia	6.1	3.4	0.5	2.1	29.5	27.7	5.2
Hungary	4.6	1.6	0.6	2.4	35.3	23.1	2.9
Latvia	6.5	3.7	0.5	2.3	31.1	24.8	5.8
Lithuania	6.6	3.4	0.5	2.7	26.3	20.6	5.2
Poland	4.3	1.6	0.6	2.1	25.1	20.0	1.8
Slovakia	4.4	1.6	0.6	2.2	38.6	26.5	3.0
Slovenia	3.9	1.6	0.5	1.8	27.4	24.3	1.7

Sources: IMF, *World Economic Outlook*; and IMF staff calculations.
[1]Growth rate in 2005–09 that corresponds to a half-life 20 percent shorter than in column 4 of Table 4.1.
[2]TFP growth is assumed to be 1.6 percent for the CE-5 and gradually declining to that level for the Baltics over 10 years.
[3]Employment rates are assumed to increase by $\frac{1}{2}$ percentage point a year and labor's share is 0.65.
[4]Calculated as a residual.

Table 4.4. Scenario 2: Speeding Up Convergence in the CEECs Through Higher Productivity Growth

	Target Growth Rate (In percent a year)[1]	Contributions (in Percent) of			Total Factor Productivity (TFP) Growth, 2000–04
		Capital[2]	Labor[3]	TFP[4]	
Czech Rep.	4.3	0.8	0.5	3.0	1.5
Estonia	6.1	1.9	0.5	3.7	5.2
Hungary	4.6	1.0	0.6	3.1	2.9
Latvia	6.5	1.4	0.5	4.5	5.8
Lithuania	6.6	1.7	0.5	4.4	5.2
Poland	4.3	1.3	0.6	2.4	1.8
Slovakia	4.4	1.0	0.6	2.9	3.0
Slovenia	3.9	1.4	0.5	2.0	1.7

Sources: IMF, *World Economic Outlook*; and IMF staff calculations.
[1]Growth rate in 2005–09 that corresponds to a half-life 20 percent shorter than in column 4 of Table 4.1.
[2]Assumes investment/GDP remains at 2000–04 averages.
[3]Employment rates are assumed to increase by $\frac{1}{2}$ percentage point a year and labor's share is 0.65.
[4]Calculated as a residual.

challenges. OECD (2004) draws attention to the labor market reforms needed to ensure a contribution of labor input similar to that assumed in the scenarios here. It also, however, recognizes that this alone will not be enough; continued rapid productivity growth is essential. Crafts and Kaiser (2004) envisage limited support from increased labor inputs or sharp rises in capital-output ratios, and therefore place an even heavier weight on productivity gains. Further to the

scope for rising capital-output ratios, Doyle, Kuijs, and Jiang (2001) caution that little is known about the quality of the capital stock in the CEECs: if depreciation rates turn out to be higher than typically assumed, investment rates needed to secure given capital contributions could be even larger than the scenarios suggest. And given the low savings rates in the CEECs, significantly larger contributions of capital to growth to compensate for shortfalls in labor or

TFP contributions would require unprecedented use of foreign savings.

While the challenge is considerable, high rates of productivity growth may indeed be possible. Caselli and Tenreyro (2005), drawing on the historical experience of Western Europe, conclude that remarkably high productivity growth has occurred in spurts. Describing Western Europe as the "quintessential convergence club," they note that "Italy first, then Spain, Greece, Portugal, and eventually Ireland all had their spurts of above average productivity growth." Labor productivity in Spain went from 65 percent of that of France to over 90 percent between the late 1950s and the early 1970s. Similarly, Ireland did not just converge but raised its productivity level to one of the highest in Europe. Since the process of integrating with Europe seems to have driven this productivity-led convergence process, they conclude that the CEECs should also be able to benefit. They point, however, to the importance of human capital development in making this possible.

V Policies and Long-Term Growth: What Can Be Learned from Other Countries?

Closing the income gap with Western Europe will require supporting policies in the CEECs. The growth accounting exercise presented in the previous section is a mechanical one. It assumes that the CEECs—at speeds varying according to their levels of development and recent histories—will continue to close their factor utilization and TFP gaps vis-à-vis Western Europe. But that is not an assumption to be made lightly. The recent debate on growth has centered on whether policies and institutions can speed up, or impede, the closing of income gaps. In other words, is the sheer existence of gaps enough to set in play forces that will close them, or must policies and other supporting conditions play a role?

This section is divided into two parts. The first summarizes the most robust conclusions of earlier studies on the determinants of long-term growth. The second updates estimates of growth models to assess the performance of the CEECs relative to their peers.

Lessons from Large Sample Studies of Long-Term Growth

A vibrant literature of empirical growth studies lends support to a variety of views on the conditions and policies that spur growth. Because economic theory does not reach clear conclusions on the conditions that best support income catch-up, researchers have looked for lessons from the experience of a large number of countries over long periods. The challenge is to sift through the voluminous (and at times contradictory) conclusions to identify the most robust influences—those that are repeatedly significant across studies covering different samples, periods, and specifications.

A good starting point is the metastudy by Sala-i-Martin, Doppelhofer, and Miller (2004; henceforth, SDM). It examines the role of 67 variables (found to be significant determinants of growth in many earlier studies) in 88 countries from 1960 to 1996. To minimize the possibility that growth may be influencing the variables thought to be the determinants, most explanatory variables are set at values of the early 1960s. The variables may be grouped in three categories:

- Geographic and socioeconomic attributes constitute 32 of the 67 variables. Some (such as prevalence of malaria and whether a country is landlocked) have an obvious bearing on the costs or availability of factor inputs, but many others (such as the East Asian and African dummy variables and ethnic variables that reflect religious composition and language attributes) have less obvious links to productive potential.

- Another 20 variables capture structural features with analytically clear links to growth potential. These include initial income per capita (lower levels create room for higher incremental product of capital and technological leapfrogging) and demographic factors such as population growth rates, fertility rates, and age composition (ceteris paribus, lower population growth means more capital accumulation per worker and hence higher productivity growth, while fertility rates and age composition determine the size of the workforce for a given population). Included in this group are institutional variables, such as measures of political rights and civil liberties.

- The remaining 15 variables are those most amenable to policy influences. Three variables are measures of education (primary schooling, higher education, and public spending on education). Another three measure openness (a variable constructed by Sachs and Warner (1995) identifying the number of years that a country had an "open" trade regime, and two indices of "outward orientation" constructed by Levine and Renelt (1992)). Six variables capture the role of the government (including the size of government and the composition of spending). Inflation and the square of inflation represent monetary conditions.

From this large set of variables, SDM identify a small range of policy variables with consistent links to growth. The cost of investment and (primary) schooling have the most robust link to growth, but greater trade openness (the number of years with an "open" trade regime and the ratio of exports and imports to GDP) and smaller government (government consumption as a share of GDP) also contribute significantly to growth. Among the structural variables (from the second grouping described above) are initial per capita GDP and, with less consistency, population growth.

These results lead to the troubling conclusion that the scope for policies to affect growth may be rather narrow or influenced by other conditions in ways that are difficult to discern. Some observers question whether the dominant influence on growth of a country's structural and institutional history leaves little role for policies (IMF, 2003; and Easterly, 2005). Alternatively, growth regressions may simply not be good at identifying policy effects on growth: they have the strength of drawing on the experience of many countries, but the weakness of largely atheoretical structures that do not account for the complexity of complementarities in growth determinants (World Bank, 2005). In other words, a certain package of policies may be good for growth, yet any policy individually may not be statistically significant. Also, the context in which policies are implemented (e.g., the stage of development or specific historical features), which cannot be fully captured in studies that cover many countries, may be critical to their effects on growth (Aghion and Howitt, 2005). Moreover, unmeasurable influences on growth may interact with measurable policies. It is worthwhile, therefore, to probe beyond the SDM metastudy for factors that may be particularly important in the CEECs.

Preparation for EU accession—especially institutional reform and opening to trade—was a key part of the context for the CEECs in the period under review. The dismantling of trade barriers increased product market competition and induced efficiency improvements. Moreover, trade has stimulated specialization, with growth effects amplified by the formation of manufacturing agglomerations.[7] The process is likely also to have added to the momentum—already established in the process of adopting the *aquis communautaire*—of institutional reform. Such an effect of trade openness is documented in Rajan and Zingales (2003) and Abiad and Mody (2005).

Evidence of the importance for growth of institutional quality is expanding. SDM consider the influence of political rights and civil liberties on growth, but do not find them significant. Other recent studies point to a large and statistically significant role of legal, political, and administrative characteristics in growth performance (IMF, 2003). In essence, institutions set the "rules of the game" that determine the incentives for production, investment, and consumption. In empirical analyses, institutions have been characterized at three levels: (1) organizational entities and regulatory frameworks (such as central bank independence and inter-

national trade agreements); (2) assessments of public institutions (quality of governance, legal protections of private property, and limits placed on politicians);[8] and (3) most ambitiously, the "deep determinants" of growth, which are essentially institutions with a long historical reach, arising, for example, from patterns of colonization and settlement and alternative legal frameworks (for example, civil versus common law).[9] Institutional quality is particularly important to investigate for the CEECs, where the institutions of central planning were a key constraint on growth prior to transition, profound institutional change has taken place in the past one-and-a-half decades, and further change will occur to conform to EU institutions.

The role of financial development in growth has generated much more controversy. Efficient financial systems should help raise investment and spur risk taking and innovation. Thus, still-underdeveloped financial markets in the CEECs may be an impediment to growth (Levine, Loayza, and Beck, 2000; and Beck, Levine, and Loayza, 2000). But most common measures of financial development (ratios of bank credit or stock market capitalization to GDP) do not have systematically significant relationships to growth. And when a significant relationship is found, it may reflect a cyclical rather than secular influence (Bosworth and Collins, 2003). Moreover, indicators of financial development and financial booms are indistinguishable. The World Bank (2005) concludes that, in the 1990s, unless financial liberalization was accompanied by prudential safeguards, it was more prone to generate crises than to spur growth. These concerns have led to an alternative way of accounting for the effect of financial development: assuming financial development is endogenous to institutions (especially for enforcing contracts), a comprehensive measure of institutional quality should capture its influence on growth (Levine, 1997).

Another continuing puzzle is the effect of fiscal policy on growth. This is a clear case where the complexity of policy interactions with growth across diverse countries is hard to specify. Leaving aside short-term Keynesian effects, government operations can affect growth through several channels. Government size is an obvious one: as governments collect a larger share of the GDP in taxes, the likelihood of disincentives to work and invest increases. But the strength of this influence depends on tax structure and the government's

---

[7]Sachs and Warner (1995) discuss these and other benefits of trade openness.

[8]Assessments of public institutions are based on indices such as those in the *International Country Risk Guide* (*ICRG*). This publication for investors includes five indices of perceptions of government stability, democratic accountability, law and order, quality of bureaucracy, and corruption in government. Keefer and Knack (1997) initiated this inquiry. Burnside and Dollar (2000); Gallup, Sachs, and Mellinger (1999); and Crafts and Kaiser (2004) find similarly robust effects of *ICRG* variables.

[9]Acemoglu, Johnson, and Robinson (2001); and Glaeser and others (2004).

ability to provide public goods. Also, the size of budget deficits, the composition of expenditures, procyclicality of revenues and expenditures, and volatility of discretionary expenditures may influence long-term growth (Aghion and Howitt, 2005; Fatás and Mihov, 2003). Most panel data studies do not find a direct effect of the size of fiscal deficits on growth: an exception is Adam and Bevan (2005) who find that growth is reduced at high budget and public debt thresholds.[10] Thus, while theory suggests channels through which deficits and government size should matter for growth, the latter is found to be the more consistent influence.

A consideration of central importance to surveillance is the role of the exchange rate regime. The strong performance of the currency board CEECs (Estonia and Lithuania) begs the question of whether such arrangements help growth. In fact, little global support exists for this view. Ghosh, Gulde, and Wolf (2002) find fixed exchange rates are associated with lower inflation: this should have an indirect benefit for growth. But if a fixed regime is not supported by sound fiscal policies, imbalances may build up, reflected in overvalued currencies and lower growth. Husain, Mody, and Rogoff (2005) find that especially in advanced economies, flexible exchange rates may enhance growth by increasing shock absorption capacity.

Updated Estimates of Growth Determinants

This section reports estimates of a relatively spare specification of a growth equation. The aim is to use up-to-date data and experiences of many countries to identify key determinants of growth for the CEECs and to form a view of growth prospects that complements the growth accounting perspective. The appendix describes the methodology and results.

Broad and narrow samples were used to establish the relevant peers. The first, a global sample with data from 125 countries, follows the conventional approach of growth studies. However, unlike standard practice, which forces a uniform speed of convergence, the estimation allows for differences in the speed of convergence across countries with different levels of institutional quality (Table 5.1). The second, a narrow sample, including 59 advanced and emerging market countries, is designed to investigate whether growth processes differ fundamentally between low-income and more advanced countries. Each exercise uses data from 1984 to 2004 in the form of five-year nonover-

lapping averages. The results from the two exercises are quite similar, although the global sample generates predictions of per capita GDP growth closer to actual performance. This suggests that as long as differences in convergence rates stemming from differences in institutional quality are accounted for, there is no need to consider advanced and less advanced country growth processes separately.

As in most other studies, the results show that factors outside the immediate control of policies have strong and robust effects.

- *A lower level of per capita income is associated with higher growth.* However, this influence depends on institutional quality. Where per capita income and institutional quality are both low, the ability to take advantage of growth opportunities is limited. This effect is captured by the composite convergence term $\beta_0 + \beta_1 \cdot InstitutionalQuality$. For most countries the composite term is negative, implying at least modest convergence. The negative coefficient on β_1 implies that as institutional quality improves, convergence accelerates (Figure 5.1).

- *More rapid population growth is associated with slower per capita GDP growth.* Common to many studies, this finding needs to be interpreted with caution. Slow population growth in the CEECs will be accompanied by changes in age structure, itself likely to have considerable but difficult-to-predict influences on growth. As in other analyses, additional demographic variables, such as dependency ratios and labor force participation rates, were not significantly correlated with growth.

- *Growth in trading partners has a positive effect on growth.* The past decade's experience raises the question of whether established patterns of trade with slow-growing partners hinders a country's growth rate, or whether countries can shift between global export markets quickly enough to take equal advantage of the fastest growing markets. Results suggest that historical trade patterns have lasting effects on growth, in line with EBRD (2004) and Arora and Vamvakidis (2005).

Several factors influenced directly or indirectly by policies have the expected significant (though generally weaker than nonpolicy variables) effects on growth.

- The *relative price of capital goods*, as a proxy for the costs of investment, is directly related to growth.

- *Years of schooling*, a generalized measure of human capital, is a robust determinant of growth in the global sample. That it is a less strong influence in the narrow (advanced and emerging market

[10]Fischer, Sahay, and Vegh (1996), for example, find that the size of fiscal deficits does not directly affect either inflation or growth once the influence of structural reforms has been taken into account.

Table 5.1. Growth Regression Estimates[1]

	Global Sample		Advanced and Emerging Market Country Sample	
Explanatory Variable	Coefficient	t-statistic	Coefficient	t-statistic
Log of per capita GDP	1.36	(1.89)	−2.27	(6.34)
Population growth	−1.46	(8.94)	−1.27	(7.42)
Partner country growth	0.62	(3.39)	0.61	(3.24)
Relative price of investment goods	−0.22	(0.84)	−0.75	(2.41)
Schooling	0.45	(2.53)	0.20	(1.40)
Openness ratio	0.01	(3.01)	0.01	(3.85)
Government taxation ratio	−0.05	(2.47)	−0.02	(1.20)
Institutional quality	0.41	(4.07)	0.03	(1.88)
Institutional quality * log of per capita GDP	−0.04	(3.86)		
Dummy, 2000–04	−10.66	(1.69)	20.93	(6.74)
Dummy, 1995–99	−11.32	(1.80)	20.31	(6.50)
Dummy, 1990–94	−10.33	(1.65)	20.96	(6.72)
Dummy, 1985–89	−11.12	(1.78)	20.51	(6.50)
Number of observations	96, 84, 52, 56		58, 51, 41, 41	
R-squared	0.47, 0.02, 0.3, 0.37		0.58, −0.17, 0.36, 0.36	

Dependent Variable: Growth Rate of Per Capita GDP (Measured at PPP)
Sample Period: Five-Year Nonoverlapping Averages, 1985–89 to 2000–04

Source: IMF staff estimates.
[1]Estimation is by seemingly unrelated regression.

Figure 5.1. Global Sample: Institutional Quality and the Speed of Convergence

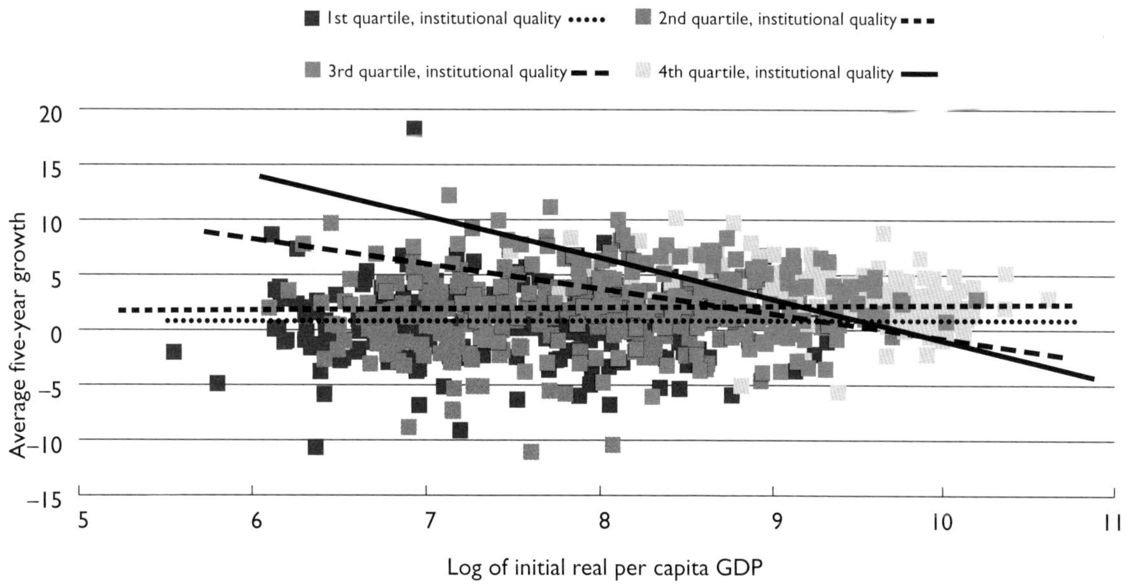

Sources: Political Risk Services, *International Country Risk Guide*; Penn World Tables; and IMF staff calculations.
Note: Observations grouped by quartile of institutional quality.

Box 5.1. Measuring Institutional Quality in the CEECs

Institutional quality in the CEECs has some important dimensions specifically related to transition. Does the *International Country Risk Guide* (*ICRG*) index pick them up? The transition index of the European Bank for Reconstruction and Development (EBRD), which reflects a variety of policy benchmarks in the transition from central planning to market mechanisms, is highly correlated with the institutional quality measure used in this paper (see figure). Components of the transition index that display particularly high correlation with the institutional quality index include some measures that were taken early in the process—enterprise restructuring and large-scale privatization—but also more contemporary policy tasks such as enhancing competition, financial sector deregulation and development, and trade liberalization (see table).

Institutional Quality and the EBRD Transition Index

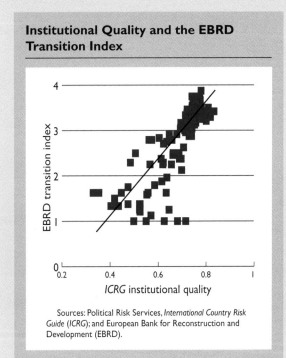

Sources: Political Risk Services, *International Country Risk Guide* (*ICRG*); and European Bank for Reconstruction and Development (EBRD).

Institutional Quality and the EBRD Transition Subindices

EBRD Subindices	Correlation with *ICRG* Composite Index
Enterprise restructuring	0.85
Competition policy	0.83
Financial liberalization	0.81
Large-enterprise privatization	0.81
Trade and foreign exchange liberalization	0.79
Securities markets	0.79
Small-scale privatization	0.61
Price liberalization	0.48

Sources: Political Risk Services, *International Country Risk Guide* (*ICRG*); European Bank for Reconstruction and Development (EBRD), and IMF staff calculations.

---

country) sample may indicate that quality of education, rather than quantity alone, becomes more important as countries advance.

- *Openness to trade*, measured as the ratio of trade to GDP, corresponds inversely to the extent of tariff and nontariff barriers and significantly helps growth. Likely channels include enhanced competition, greater specialization, and pressure to improve the business climate.

- Fiscal policy is found to influence growth through the *size of government*—larger governments apparently pull growth down. The size of the budget deficit was not found to have an independent effect on growth across countries.

- The *ICRG* composite index, as a proxy for the *quality of institutions*, has a significant positive effect on growth and is a key factor in differentiating the speed of catch-up as between advanced and low-income countries. As indicators of financial development (private credit/GDP, stock market capitalization/GDP) were not found to be significant, this variable is likely to be indirectly picking up effects of financial development on growth. For the CEECs, the variable is also correlated with progress in shifting from central planning to market mechanisms (Box 5.1).

- *Monetary conditions* were found to have a significant effect on growth through the influence of inflation relative to a threshold of 50 percent (rates higher than the threshold hurt growth). The exchange rate regime was not found to have a significant effect.[11]

---

[11]Results excluding inflation are shown in the box and used in the rest of the analysis, because omitting the variable had virtually no effect on other estimates and inflation in the CEECs is well below the threshold.

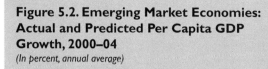

Figure 5.2. Emerging Market Economies: Actual and Predicted Per Capita GDP Growth, 2000–04
(In percent, annual average)

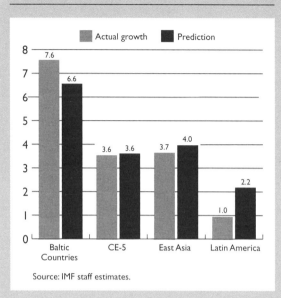

Source: IMF staff estimates.

The estimates predict actual per capita growth rates during 2000–04 well in the CE-5 but less well in two of the Baltic countries (Figures 5.2 and 5.3). Using the results of the global sample model, predicted annual per capita growth rates for 2000–04 at about 3½ percent to 4 percent for the CE-5 and almost 7 percent for Lithuania are close to actual growth rates. For Estonia and Latvia, however, the predicted growth rates of about 6½ percent are below actual growth rates of almost 8 percent. The model's higher growth prediction for Lithuania vis-à-vis Estonia and Latvia can be traced to two factors: smaller government size and a low per capita income in Lithuania (combined with better institutions relative to Latvia). The underprediction of growth in Estonia and Latvia and the prediction of reduced growth rates in all the Baltic countries as the income gap vis-à-vis the euro area diminishes raises questions about continued performance at current rates.

Interpreting the Strengths and Weaknesses of the CEECs

During 2000–04, exogenous conditions favored growth in the CEECs but overall policy conditions were mixed relative to East Asia—a useful comparator (Figure 5.4). Despite higher initial per capita income in the CE-5 than in East Asia, slower population growth gave the CE-5 an edge of between 1–2 percentage points

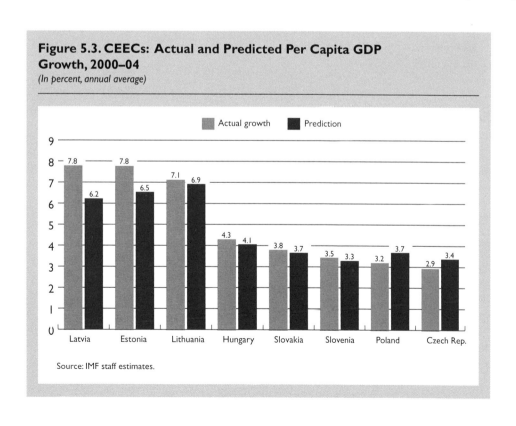

Figure 5.3. CEECs: Actual and Predicted Per Capita GDP Growth, 2000–04
(In percent, annual average)

Source: IMF staff estimates.

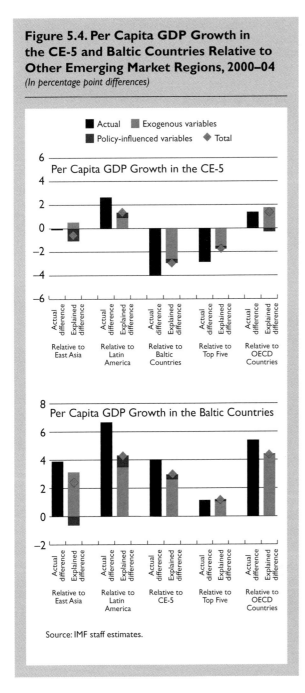

Figure 5.4. Per Capita GDP Growth in the CE-5 and Baltic Countries Relative to Other Emerging Market Regions, 2000–04
(In percentage point differences)

- ■ Actual
- ■ Policy-influenced variables
- ■ Exogenous variables
- ◆ Total

Per Capita GDP Growth in the CE-5

Relative to East Asia / Relative to Latin America / Relative to Baltic Countries / Relative to Top Five / Relative to OECD Countries

(Actual difference / Explained difference)

Per Capita GDP Growth in the Baltic Countries

Relative to East Asia / Relative to Latin America / Relative to CE-5 / Relative to Top Five / Relative to OECD Countries

(Actual difference / Explained difference)

Source: IMF staff estimates.

average, had smaller governments, higher educational attainment, and greater openness (the latter owing fully to Hong Kong SAR and Singapore), but the CE-5 on average had better scores for institutional development. The Baltics are less disadvantaged vis-à-vis East Asia with respect to their "policy" package, despite lower average institutional development, and substantial gains in institutional quality in the Baltic countries in the run-up to EU accession have likely narrowed this disadvantage.

About three-fourths of the difference between growth in the Baltic countries and the CE-5 reflected identifiable differences in conditions and policies. Relatively low per capita incomes in Lithuania and Latvia created a sizable catch-up potential, while population growth was even lower in the Baltics than in the CE-5. The Baltic countries' export markets—in which Nordic countries and Russia feature prominently—are growing fast, providing a substantial leg up from an already-strong outward orientation. Policies present a mixed picture. The Baltics have the advantage in schooling, openness, and government size, but this was offset by an apparently higher price of investment and slightly weaker institutional quality. The models do not explain about 1½ percentage points of the recent growth in Estonia and Latvia, which could reflect a bounce back from the sharp effects of the Russian crisis in 1998 or an underestimate of the effects of improvements in the business climate, including in the cost of investment. Without a clear understanding, however, of the basis for recent strong growth, particularly in Estonia and Latvia, its durability cannot be taken for granted.

Trends and Prospects

The CEECs have improved policies in several dimensions that should contribute to growth potential. Some of the major efforts were undertaken during the transition from the planned system even as large output losses occurred. In particular, privatization and the development of complementary market institutions improved sharply measures of institutional quality in the early 1990s (Table 5.2). Since then, continued improvements are reflected in falling relative prices of investment, greater openness, increased years of schooling, and smaller governments.

But pressures have increased to do more just to maintain the same rate of growth. As per capita incomes have increased, the easy catch-up potential has declined. In particular, the possibilities for productivity gains through more efficient use of existing capital and reallocation of resources to higher-productivity growth sectors are increasingly limited. Thus, using the estimation results and assuming that explanatory variables remain at their 2004 levels, growth rates of 3½–4 percent a year are predicted in the CE-5 (Figure 5.5). On the same basis, growth rates in the Baltics are predicted to

each year. About half of this advantage, however, was taken away by slower export market growth. In contrast, for the Baltics, lower per capita incomes, lower population growth, and rapid growth in export markets (at the same pace as for East Asian economies) resulted in a substantial advantage on structural characteristics vis-à-vis East Asia. The CE-5 had a policy disadvantage relative to East Asia, accounting for lower growth rates by about 1 percentage point a year: East Asia, on

Table 5.2. Evolution of Growth Determinants in the CEECs, 1989–2004

		Schooling[1]	Relative Price of Investment[2]	Openness[3]	Institutional Quality[4]	Government Size[5]	Partner Growth[6]
Czech Rep.	1989				69.38		1.12
	1994	2.93	1.38	103.64	78.71	47.00	2.59
	1999	2.97	1.28	123.17	75.90	39.20	2.24
	2004	3.25	1.23	158.84	76.34	41.40	2.48
Hungary	1989	2.15	1.57	72.85	64.50		1.35
	1994	2.28	1.28	67.72	73.04	44.30	2.46
	1999	2.43	1.18	108.48	75.79	44.40	2.19
	2004	2.59	1.20	113.75	75.77	44.40	2.36
Poland	1989	2.08	1.67	32.74	52.25		0.41
	1994	2.21	1.19	45.14	75.13	47.40	2.11
	1999	2.32	1.19	58.64	77.93	44.90	2.51
	2004	2.43	1.09	89.09	75.03	40.90	2.54
Slovakia	1989		1.36	57.48	69.38		0.67
	1994		1.34	118.45	71.42	51.70	2.18
	1999	2.93	1.30	128.42	74.58	49.80	2.21
	2004	3.05	1.21	162.23	75.32	37.40	2.48
Slovenia	1989						−0.09
	1994	3.29	1.03	114.82			3.33
	1999	3.67	1.02	109.65	79.03	44.30	2.54
	2004	4.00	1.00	120.43	79.40	45.40	2.72
Estonia	1989						−2.18
	1994	3.32	1.96	171.47		44.00	2.76
	1999	3.43	1.98	158.93	73.16	39.10	3.73
	2004	3.65	2.05	164.48	75.17	37.90	3.28
Lithuania	1989						−2.10
	1994	3.32	2.24	116.77		34.20	2.33
	1999	3.53	1.51	89.80	73.29	37.30	3.87
	2004	3.79	1.60	115.57	75.68	32.10	3.42
Latvia	1989						−1.05
	1994	3.14	2.77	90.28		37.10	2.76
	1999	3.41	2.18	97.97	71.57	36.90	3.38
	2004	3.67	2.29	106.06	76.11	35.30	3.15

Source: IMF staff calculations.

[1]Average years of higher education in the population. Hungary and Poland are from the Barro-Lee education data set; for the other countries, estimates based on secondary and tertiary school enrollments (World Bank, *World Development Indicators*).

[2]Ratio of investment deflator to GDP deflator (Penn World Tables (PWT)); last observation is for 2000.

[3]Sum of exports and imports, relative to GDP, all measured in current prices (PWT; and IMF, *World Economic Outlook*).

[4]Composite index (0–100, higher is better) (Political Risk Services, *International Country Risk Guide*).

[5]General government revenue in percent of GDP (Eurostat).

[6]Trade-weighted partner country growth (IMF, *World Economic Outlook*).

be 5½ percent to 6 percent a year, substantially below their actual growth in 2000–04, unless the recent over-performance is in fact based on underlying strengths not captured in the model.

Mapping how underlying policies will influence the contributions of capital and labor inputs and TFP is not straightforward. In fact, there are good reasons to expect all the policies considered to influence invest-ment, labor supply and demand, and TFP growth. But exploratory work, shown in the appendix, suggests that schooling is more important for productivity growth, and that institutional quality increases the catch-up in productivity growth more than the catch-up in capital per head. Trade openness, presumably through its effects on competition and specialization, steps up investment and accelerates productivity growth. That said, raising employment ratios to at least the EU average is likely to be a sine qua non for the catch-up. In turn, this will require a variety of labor market measures, not explic-itly included in the empirical exercise.

Figure 5.5. CEECs: Predicted Per Capita GDP Growth, 2005–09
(In percent, PPP, annual average)

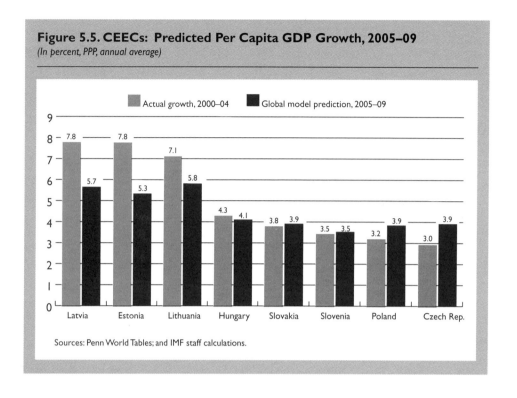

Sources: Penn World Tables; and IMF staff calculations.

VI   European Integration: Opportunities for Growth

Formal membership in the EU and, prospectively, the euro area critically differentiates the CEECs from other emerging market countries. An obvious and quantifiable benefit comes from large transfers from the EU—which for the 2000–06 budget period are in the range of 2 percent to 3 percent of GDP for the CEECs. Probably of greater importance will be the potential for larger private capital inflows as markets and institutions become more integrated. Against these influences, however, the European market may continue to grow more slowly than others—a pattern that in the past appears to have constrained growth in the CE-5 relative to other emerging market country groupings. How best to use potential benefits from European integration is key for CEEC growth prospects.

Perhaps the largest benefit from European integration will come from the scope provided for easing the savings constraint on growth. Not only will consumers want to smooth consumption in anticipation of future income growth, but also the potential for productive deployment of foreign savings in the CEECs is large. Lipschitz, Lane, and Mourmouras (2002 and 2005) emphasize that savings rates are generally low by emerging market standards, while low capital-labor ratios imply high marginal returns to capital.[12] Sizable use of foreign savings is already reflected in large current account deficits (between 8 percent and 12 percent of GDP in the Baltic countries, for example), but the Lipschitz, Lane, and Mourmouras estimates suggest that capital flows to the CEECs could be even larger. Why has this not happened on a larger scale? Currency risk is an obvious hindrance, but Lucas (1990) also points to obstacles to technology transfer and shortcomings in institutional quality. As the convergence of institutions toward EU norms proceeds and the CEECs eliminate currency risk by adopting the euro, the use of foreign savings could be far greater than in other emerging market countries.

The impetus to growth in the CEECs from foreign savings is already evident. Estimates of the growth equation (developed in the previous section) including foreign savings bear out other evidence that growing financial integration in the EU has weakened the constraint of domestic savings on investment—the so-called Feldstein-Horioka puzzle.[13] The estimates (Box 6.1 and the appendix) bear out heuristic evidence that, within the EU, countries with lower per capita income and more rapid growth have tended to make greater use of foreign savings, which in turn have supported higher growth not only directly but also by increasing the speed of convergence (Figure 6.1). That is, foreign savings have been a particularly important spur to growth in countries with lower per capita incomes.

Both FDI and other financial flows have contributed to higher growth. Decomposing current account financing into FDI and other financial flows in the estimated equation shows that FDI has both a direct effect on growth (consistent with evidence in Mody and Murshid, 2005) and a medium-term effect through increasing the speed of convergence. This seems consistent with the special importance of FDI in facilitating privatization and restructuring during 1995–2002. More recently, FDI/GDP has fallen in some countries as privatization-related inflows have winded down, while non-FDI flows have increased (Figure 6.2). These flows have also have had a strong and robust effect on the speed of convergence, suggesting that the loosening of financial constraints and not just the transfer of technology through FDI is playing a role in speeding up the convergence process.

Accounting for the interplay between growth and the use of foreign savings allows a benchmarking of recent current account deficits. The growth predictions from the augmented model are in line with those from the growth regressions in Section V for most of the CEECs. Varying degrees of underprediction of the rapid growth in the Baltics in recent years persists (Figure 6.3). At the same time, the estimates suggest that the relatively large current account deficits in Latvia and Lithuania have

---

[12]On the assumption that TFP in these countries is 70 percent of German TFP, they estimate that marginal product of capital in the CEECs excluding Slovenia is between 1.7 to 10.6 times the marginal product of capital in Germany. Adjusting their estimates for the lower TFP ratios in Table 4.2 still leaves most of the CEECs with marginal products of capital 1.2 to 6.3 times that in Germany.

[13]See Blanchard and Giavazzi (2002) for similar results for the 15 member countries of the EU (henceforth, EU-15) prior to 2004.

Box 6.1. International Financial Linkages and Growth

Countries with relatively low income and those growing rapidly can be expected to attract international capital to take advantage of the higher marginal product of capital and growth opportunities. This process is modeled in two equations, estimated simultaneously. The current account is a function of the country's per capita income and GDP growth rate in the previous year. In addition, a higher dependency ratio is predicted to lower national savings and, all else equal, increase the current account deficit. Growth is a function of per capita GDP in the previous year (allowing, as before, for the possibility of catch-up and also for the short-term tendency for mean-reversion). Because the focus here is on short-term dynamics, some of the long-term growth determinants used in the previous section are excluded. Higher schooling rates continue to be related to higher growth; more rapid population growth is related (though not statistically significantly) to lower per capita income growth. Other variables did not change sufficiently from one year to another to show a material influence.

The augmented growth regression is estimated on EU-25 data from 1975 to 2004, where the new member states are included from 1995 onward. We find that current account deficits support growth and allow for faster convergence for low-income countries. Further analysis, shown in columns 2 to 4 of the table, indicates that this is not simply driven by FDI: non-FDI financial flows also have a significant beneficial effect.

Financial Integration and Growth Regressions

	Dependent Variable: Growth in Real GDP Per Capita			
Log of per capita GDP[1]	−4.76	−3.00	−4.01	−4.09
	[4.17]***	[2.75]***	[3.70]***	[3.73]***
Schooling	0.25	0.28	0.29	0.29
	[2.59]***	[2.89]***	[3.01]***	[3.01]**
Population growth	−0.06	−0.15	−0.13	0.12
	[0.22]	[0.62]	[0.52]	[0.52]
Current account deficit	3.68			
	[3.25]***			
Log of per capita GDP*current account deficit	−0.39			
	[3.31]***			
Net FDI		0.11		2.42
		[3.74]***		[2.70]***
Log of per capita GDP*FDI				−0.25
				[2.73]***
Non-FDI flows			−0.08	3.53
			[3.78]***	[5.53]***
Log of per capita GDP*non-FDI flows				−0.37
				[5.62]***
Number of observations	503	503	503	503
R-squared	0.49	0.47	0.47	0.50

Source: Authors' calculations.

Note: Estimation by three-stage least squares. *, **, and *** indicate significance at 10 percent, 5 percent, and 1 percent levels, respectively.

[1]The coefficient on income is time-varying; the parameter estimate for 2004 is shown.

been in the range consistent with per capita income; in contrast, in Estonia, the current account deficit—at over 12 percent of GDP in 2003 and 2004—was substantially higher than the mean prediction (Figure 6.4). In the CE-5, Poland has relied less than predicted on foreign savings, consistent with growth lower than predicted. At the other extreme, Hungary's sizable current account deficit is near the large end of the predicted band, while actual growth is at the lower end of its predicted band: this suggests that inflows have not stimulated short-term growth, perhaps increasing vulnerability.

Rapid growth along with large-scale use of foreign savings inevitably produces conditions commonly associated with heightened vulnerabilities to financial shocks. Similarities between some of the CEECs and East Asia prior to 1997 underscore the immediacy of these concerns (Figure 6.5): current account deficits are large; credit growth rates (much in foreign currency) are rapid; and external debt ratios are high, particularly in the Baltics and Hungary. Reserve cover of short-term debt is, however, generally high, except in the Baltics, where Estonia and Lithuania are constrained by cur-

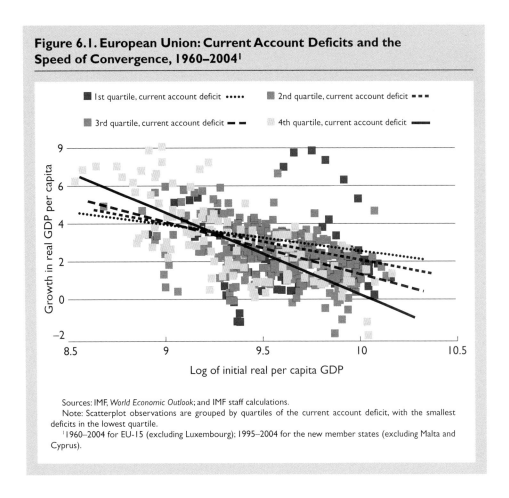

Figure 6.1. European Union: Current Account Deficits and the Speed of Convergence, 1960–2004[1]

■ 1st quartile, current account deficit ••••• 　 ■ 2nd quartile, current account deficit ▪▪▪

■ 3rd quartile, current account deficit ▬ ▬ 　 ■ 4th quartile, current account deficit ▬▬▬

Sources: IMF, *World Economic Outlook*; and IMF staff calculations.

Note: Scatterplot observations are grouped by quartiles of the current account deficit, with the smallest deficits in the lowest quartile.

[1] 1960–2004 for EU-15 (excluding Luxembourg); 1995–2004 for the new member states (excluding Malta and Cyprus).

rency boards. Notably also, the financial and public sectors in the CEECs conform to a rather high standard of transparency and quality of governance (Figure 6.6)—features that should help markets to understand, price, and monitor risks more effectively. That said, Lipschitz, Lane, and Mourmouras (2002 and 2005) point to discontinuities in the response of risk premia to changing circumstances of borrowers as a sign of uneven or insufficient market appraisal of risk. Thus, they predict that excessive exposure, sudden stops, and crises are endemic to highly integrated countries with large differences in returns on capital.

Critical for the CEECs is whether the opportunities for institutional and financial integration with Western Europe change the nature of these risks. Since this paper examines the requirements for a rapid catch-up in the CEECs, a full consideration of vulnerabilities—

the central focus of bilateral and multilateral surveillance in these countries—is beyond its scope. But the two are closely related: to the extent that faster growth involves extensive use of foreign savings, signs of vulnerabilities will emerge, but how much of a concern they are depends in part on how productively foreign savings are used—that is, how strong the catch-up is. The evidence here suggests that the opportunities for institutional integration—especially, prospectively, the elimination of currency risk through the adoption of the euro—could fundamentally reduce the domestic savings constraint for the CEECs and, provided policies to support growth are right, secure a faster catch-up than is possible, safely, in other emerging market countries. Judging where the limit to this process is, especially prior to euro adoption, will be the major challenge for IMF surveillance.

Figure 6.2. CEECs: FDI and Non-FDI Financing of Current Account Deficit
(In percent of GDP)

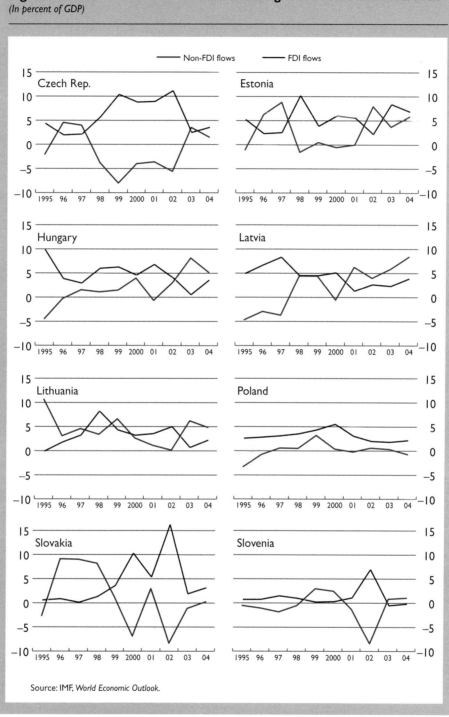

Source: IMF, *World Economic Outlook.*

Figure 6.3. CEECs: Predicted Versus Actual Per Capita GDP Growth
(In percent, PPP)

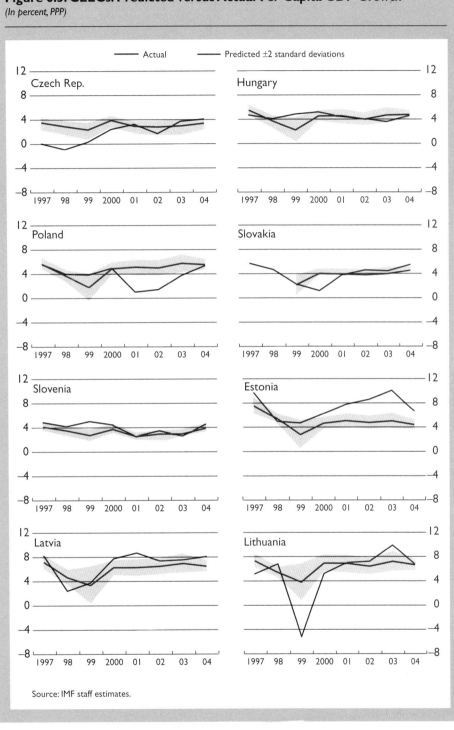

Source: IMF staff estimates.

Figure 6.4. CEECs: Actual Versus Predicted Current Account Balance
(In percent of GDP)

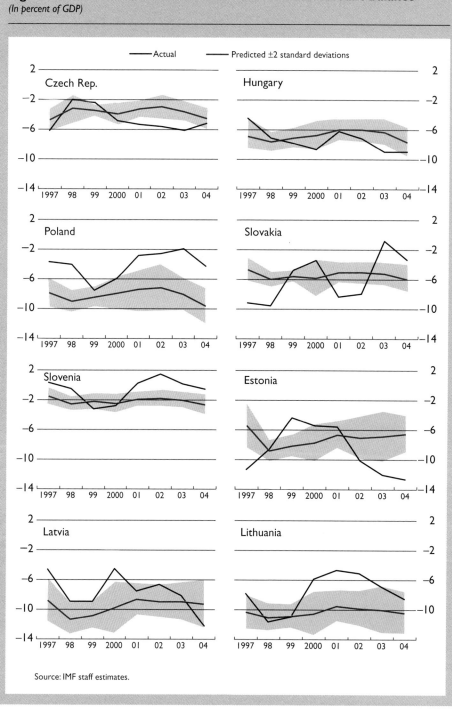

Source: IMF staff estimates.

**Figure 6.5. CEECs in 2005 and East Asia in 1996:
Selected Vulnerability Indicators**

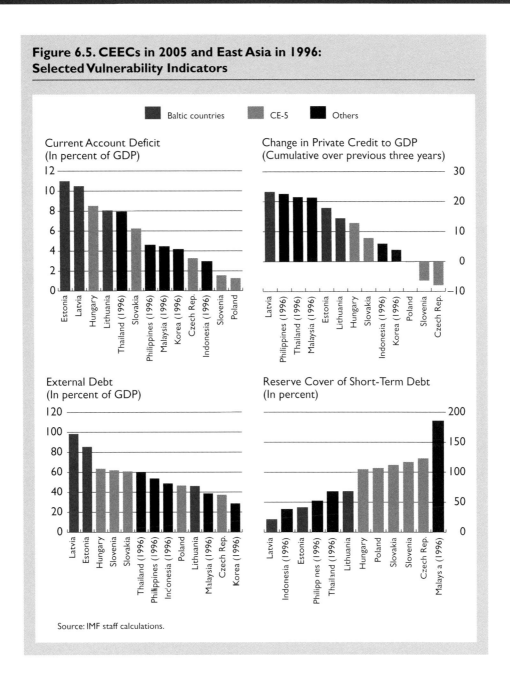

Source: IMF staff calculations.

Figure 6.6. The CEECs and East Asia: Selected Governance Indicators

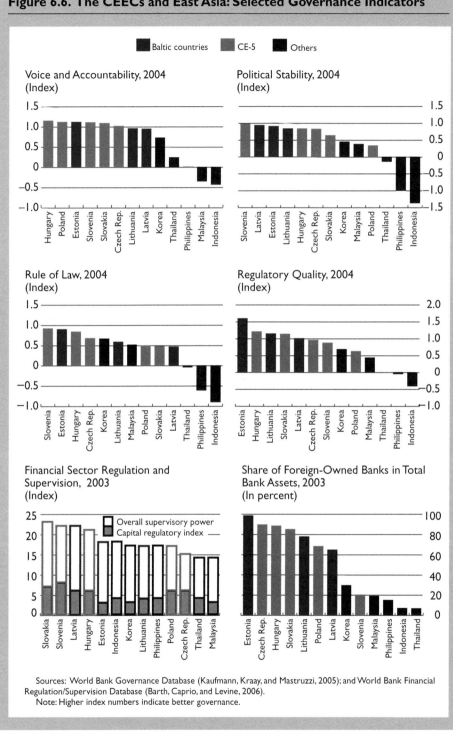

Sources: World Bank Governance Database (Kaufmann, Kraay, and Mastruzzi, 2005); and World Bank Financial Regulation/Supervision Database (Barth, Caprio, and Levine, 2006).

Note: Higher index numbers indicate better governance.

VII Implications for IMF Surveillance

A medium- to long-term perspective on growth will be a necessary complement to the short-term concerns prominent in surveillance. The CEECs, having emerged from the low-growth era of central planning, have in EU membership a unique opportunity to catch up to advanced country levels. But even when pursued with focus and determination, catching up will be a long-drawn process. Surveillance must therefore help guide a series of reinforcing measures that cumulate in sustained growth, while containing vulnerabilities inherent in the catching-up process. Ultimately, growth mitigates vulnerabilities.

The review of growth prospects in the CEECs suggests several directions for this aspect of surveillance. Broadly, these are increasing employment, fostering productivity growth, and managing risks inherent in greater use of foreign savings, including through euro adoption. Although mapping the variables identified in this study to specific policies is not straightforward, several directions for IMF advice are indicated: the particular measures relevant to a country will reflect its history and institutional structure.

Labor Absorption

The spread of gainful employment will be a central challenge. After employment rates fell sharply during transition, they have at best stabilized at rates that are low relative to other emerging market countries. It seems likely that rapid structural change has created unusually high structural inactivity that may reverse as the pace of job destruction slows. Moreover, by some conventional measures (such as employment protection legislation, unemployment benefits, and the degree of unionization) labor markets in the CEECs are not notably inflexible. Nevertheless, achieving the ½ percentage point a year increase envisaged in the growth scenarios in Section IV will be a major hurdle. OECD (2004), Schiff and others (2006), and Choueiri (2005) identify measures that will be an integral part of growth-enhancing policies.

Broadly, and it must be recognized that labor market characteristics and problems vary widely, these studies identify a few major priorities.

- *Restrictions on dismissals and on temporary employment,* while not standouts among OECD countries, are still sufficiently cumbersome in some countries as to limit the growth of labor demand.

- *Fiscal disincentives to labor supply and demand* are substantial in some CEECs. Payments to inactive persons—disability benefits, social assistance, and, to a lesser extent, unemployment benefits—are significant disincentives to job search and excessive burdens on government finances. The tax wedge (personal income tax and social security contributions) is high in some CEECs. Joint action on these problems can improve incentives to work without worsening fiscal accounts.

- *Regional mobility* has been hampered by social transfers, low costs of living in high-unemployment areas, and rigidities in the housing, especially in the rental, markets.

- *Skill mismatches* seem to be a significant problem in some CEECs, indicating an important role for better tailoring educational systems to labor market needs.

Closing the Productivity Gap

Raising CEEC productivity to EU levels will depend on raising capital-labor ratios through high investment and improving the efficiency of resource use. The analysis in this paper identifies several influences on such objectives that are directly and indirectly related to policies. Some, such as improving education, are rather clearly outside the scope of IMF surveillance. Others, such as openness to trade and keeping the relative cost of investment low, are ones on which the CEECs already score rather well. However, three—sustaining low inflation, containing the size of government, and improving institutions—are squarely within the mandate of IMF surveillance.

The CEECs have all achieved inflation rates well below thresholds identified as harmful for growth prospects. Low inflation expectations should provide support for keeping this record intact. Nevertheless, especially for the countries that are most successful in

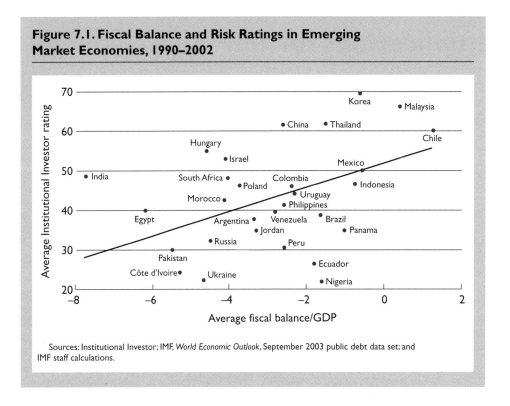

Figure 7.1. Fiscal Balance and Risk Ratings in Emerging Market Economies, 1990–2002

Sources: Institutional Investor; IMF, *World Economic Outlook*, September 2003 public debt data set; and IMF staff calculations.

achieving a rapid catch-up, price pressures can emerge quickly. A key role of surveillance is to anticipate any pickup in inflation and help tailor monetary, fiscal, and wage policies to curtailing it.

Arriving at a size of government that supports growth prospects is likely to be a bigger challenge. The results in this study suggest that larger governments are associated with slower growth. This effect can work through various inefficiencies: a heavy tax burden that produces disincentives to work or invest, or spending that runs ahead of government's ability to deliver public goods and services efficiently. Thus, notwithstanding evidence that governments in some advanced countries can effectively supply public goods on a large scale, it seems likely that the CEECs, with their legacy of inefficiencies associated with central planning, will benefit from maintaining or achieving relatively small governments. And because infrastructure needs to support growth are likely to be large, the focus will need to be on constraining current spending.

A more difficult question is how the size of fiscal deficits influences growth. In general, little evidence exists of a robust direct link between budget deficits, on the one hand, and growth, investment, or inflation, on the other.[14] However, this may reflect the fact that even thresholds beyond which deficits might affect growth

will depend importantly on initial debt ratios, the history of inflation, and the time-specific appetite for risk in local and global financial markets. Indeed, insofar as fiscal deficits are often the source of currency crises with attendant output costs, fiscal sustainability must be at the core of a sound growth strategy. The correlation between risk premia on interest rates and the size of deficits is a manifestation of this constraint (Figure 7.1).[15] But the fiscal stance is likely to play a broader role in the CEECs—restraining the pace of demand growth in countries that get the underlying conditions for rapid convergence right. For some CEECs already, fiscal balances that are substantially stronger than considerations of debt sustainability alone would require have become necessary to contain overheating pressures resulting from large capital inflows, currency appreciation, and rapid bank credit growth.

A third broad issue is to nurture institutions—many at the macroeconomic level—that underpin growth. The measure of institutional development used in this study is broad—a composite of measures of government stability, democratic accountability, law and order, quality of bureaucracy, and corruption in government. As such it indicates the importance of institutions for growth,

---

[14]See, for example, Harberger (2003) and Edwards (2003).

[15]Consistent with this risk interpretation, Adam and Bevan (2005) find that deficits hurt growth only if they exceed 1.5 percent of GDP. Moreover, larger deficits are more harmful to growth the higher the public debt.

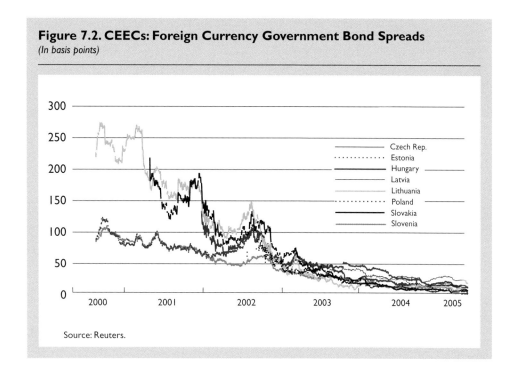

Figure 7.2. CEECs: Foreign Currency Government Bond Spreads
(In basis points)

Source: Reuters.

but does not point to specific measures that are particularly important. That said, other literature, together with the findings of Article IV consultations, points to five institutional areas with significant macroeconomic dimensions that should be the focus of structural policy efforts: financial supervision and prudential control, judicial institutions and efficient protection of property rights, the scope for corruption, costs of doing business, and product market competition.

Use of Foreign Savings

Use of foreign savings will continue to feature prominently in surveillance. The results from this study point to the importance of recognizing the role of foreign savings in contributing to growth and avoiding rules of thumb on "safe" maximum current account deficits. The lower-income, rapidly growing economies have run large current account deficits and the associated capital flows have contributed to the strength of growth. Yet obviously large net inflows, alongside sizable reductions in country risk premia (Figure 7.2), and rapid increases in foreign-exchange-denominated bank credit, raise concerns about whether financial markets are adequately assessing risks.

A key issue will therefore be to discern when large current account deficits are constructively facilitating the catch-up and when they pose undue vulnerabilities. The evidence in this study suggests that substantial use of foreign savings in most of the CEECs is within a range consistent with their strong growth rates. But exceptions exist, and judgments even in the apparently clearer-cut cases can be subject to considerable uncertainty. Indeed, the CEECs are likely to exemplify the tension between the role of large inflows in supporting a rapid catch-up and their contribution to vulnerabilities stemming from rising external debt/GDP, strong appreciation, rapid credit growth, and balance sheet mismatches. It will be important to balance acceptance of large changes that accompany rapid catch-up with vigilance in identifying when such changes involve excessive vulnerabilities.

Euro Adoption

A central question for the region is how the adoption of the euro could affect growth prospects and, specifically, the risks in large-scale use of foreign savings. As small open economies with sufficient flexibility to absorb asymmetric shocks, the CEECs should benefit considerably from adopting a major international currency. Gains from euro adoption fall into three categories: increased trade, greater policy discipline, and lower risk premia and the related scope for larger use of foreign savings.

Considerable empirical work suggests that joining a currency union raises overall trade and, presumably through efficiency gains from greater competition, output growth (Schadler and others, 2005). These studies find that upon joining a currency union, countries increase trade with other countries in the union while trade with countries outside the union does not decrease—and may even increase. Gravity models of Economic and Monetary Union suggest gains of 6–15 percent, after only five years of its initiation (Faruqee, 2004). One controversy about these findings concerns whether they adequately differentiate trade gains owing to euro adoption from those owing to ongoing economic integration with Europe (Gomes and others, 2004). Faruqee finds, however, that gains from euro adoption differed across countries, with the gains being largest where existing international production networks were already in place.

A dilemma for the CE-5 will be balancing the benefits and costs of diversifying trade. The findings in this paper suggest that increased trade and openness to trade—owing in no small part to EU accession—have been a major impetus to growth in the CEECs. Those growing trade ties have also enhanced the cyclical convergence of the CE-5 in particular with the euro area—a key optimal currency area criterion. Yet the strength of the CE-5 trade ties with the relatively slow-growing euro area core has also meant that the direct benefit from trade has been less in the CE-5 than in the Baltics with their orientation toward the faster-growing Nordic countries and Russia. Geography and history may play such strong roles that significant diversification would be difficult, but the advantages of closer integration with the euro area core versus greater trade diversification to capture benefits from faster-growing markets should be considered.

The potential for increased policy discipline as a result of joining the euro area is uncertain. By providing an external anchor, the prospect of euro adoption and, subsequently, actual membership can foster fiscal discipline and spur structural reforms to increase economic flexibility. Although causality is difficult to ascertain, the boost to growth for some current euro area members has been in some cases impressive. In contrast, other countries have fallen victim to short-term incentives to meet the Maastricht criteria, and, without addressing underlying fiscal and structural problems, have ended up with overvalued parities adding to the negative effects of rigidities on growth.

The reduction in risk premia—in the run-up to and following the introduction of the euro—is a third potentially strong advantage for growth. Most CEECs have already seen their risk premia drop to levels that are among the lowest in emerging market countries. Further gains, while not insignificant, will therefore be small. Of perhaps greater importance for growth will be the scope for increased use of foreign savings as financial integration increases and the risks—particularly those associated with foreign exchange exposure— diminish. In principle, this would allow a delinking of domestic savings and investment beyond that already seen in some of the CEECs.

The timing and conditions of euro adoption are likely to have major effects on growth prospects, especially in countries that now have significant exchange rate flexibility. The experiences of current euro area members point to three critical steps prior to joining the euro area (Schadler and others, 2005). First, choosing a conversion rate compatible with strong export performance is crucial. While upward adjustments through inflation are not particularly difficult, downward adjustments would take a major toll even in the most flexible economies. Second, entering from a position of sound macroeconomic policies—particularly with fiscal deficit and debt ratios well below the Maastricht limits of 3 percent and 60 percent of GDP, respectively—will protect against the need for procyclical fiscal policies and difficulties in the event of financial shocks. Third, bolstering mechanisms for economic flexibility will help secure the ability to adjust to shocks and respond to opportunities from any changes in comparative advantage within the euro area.

Appendix   Growth Regressions and Data Description

Panel Growth Regressions

The analysis of growth performance covered a broad range of countries over the period 1984–2004. While, in principle, the regressions attempted to cover the set of developed and developing economies listed in Table A1, gaps in the data reduced the number actually included in the regression by an extent that depended on the specification. In particular, because more data were available for recent years, the sample size increased over time. The dependent variable in the regressions are growth rates of real per capita GDP in PPP terms, calculated over nonoverlapping five-year periods (e.g., 2000–04, 1995–99, 1990–94), providing time-series as well as cross-sectional variation.

Variables used for explaining growth were influenced by recent findings on the robustness of growth determinants and the context of the CEECs. The robustness of growth influences was judged primarily by the results in SDM (2004). In addition to initial income per capita, other controls suggested by neoclassical growth models were population growth, the price of investment, and human capital accumulation (proxied by the average years of higher education). As discussed in the main text, additional controls in the benchmark regression include partner country growth, openness to trade, the size of government (proxied by tax revenues to GDP), and a measure of institutional quality. Further details on the construction of these variables can be found in the data description below.

One novel feature of the growth regressions is the inclusion of an interaction term between institutional quality and per capita income. Background studies for this paper found that institutional quality affects not only the steady-state level of income but also the speed at which countries converge to the steady state. This can be seen in Figure 5.1, which groups observations into quartiles of institutional quality and plots the best-fit lines through each quartile. Better institutional quality is associated not only with higher steady state incomes (reflected in the best-fit lines shifting up) but also with a higher speed of convergence (reflected in the steeper slopes, so that countries with superior institutions move more quickly toward their steady-state income levels).

Following Barro and Sala-i-Martin (2004), we use the seemingly unrelated regression procedure to estimate the growth model. This procedure allows for country random effects that are correlated over time; that is, it estimates each five-year period as a cross section but controls for the possibility that the residuals in each cross-section regression are correlated, as they are likely to be in these growth regressions. Our results, however, are robust to using different econometric specifications, including simple random effects and cluster ordinary least squares where standard errors are adjusted for within-group correlation. As an additional robustness check, which also sheds substantive light on differences across country groups, the regressions were run on different subsamples—developing countries, emerging market countries, and advanced economies—to assess whether parameter estimates change systematically across the groups.

Regressions for different country groups (reported in Table A2) illustrate variations across the groups using a core set of explanatory variables. These variables behave directionally the same way across country groups, but the size and significance of coefficients are quite different. Thus, there is support both for commonality of growth drivers and for the dissimilarity of their potency. Of interest is the finding on variations in conditional convergence across country groups. In the group of non-emerging-market developing countries, even conditional convergence seems to be absent. In contrast, emerging and advanced economies are characterized by both absolute and conditional convergence. For this reason, when we use the global sample for analyzing growth, it is important to make allowance for variations in convergence rates. Other growth determinants similarly operate with differing force across country groups.

The two benchmark regressions are presented in Table A3. So as not to introduce a proliferation of results, we worked toward two "benchmark" regressions: a suitably modified "global" regression, which deals with variations in convergence rates across countries, and an advanced economy–emerging market regression, which drops developing countries to ensure that the results are not being driven solely by low-income countries. As we report below, both regressions give qualitatively similar

Table A1. Global Sample of Economies

Albania	Guinea	Panama
Algeria	Guinea-Bissau	Papua New Guinea
Angola	Haiti	Paraguay
Argentina	Honduras	Peru
Armenia	Hong Kong SAR	Philippines
Australia	Hungary	Poland
Austria	India	Portugal
Azerbaijan	Indonesia	Romania
Bangladesh	Iran, I.R. of	Russia
Belarus	Ireland	Saudi Arabia
Belgium	Israel	Senegal
Bolivia	Italy	Serbia and Montenegro
Botswana	Jamaica	Sierra Leone
Brazil	Japan	Singapore
Bulgaria	Jordan	Slovakia
Burkina Faso	Kazakhstan	Slovenia
Cameroon	Kenya	South Africa
Canada	Korea	Spain
Chile	Kuwait	Sri Lanka
China	Latvia	Sudan
Colombia	Lebanon	Sweden
Congo, Dem. Rep. of	Libya	Switzerland
Congo, Rep. of	Lithuania	Syrian Arab Rep.
Costa Rica	Madagascar	Taiwan Province of China
Croatia	Malawi	Tanzania
Czech Republic	Malaysia	Thailand
Côte d'Ivoire	Mali	Togo
Denmark	Mexico	Trinidad and Tobago
Dominican Rep.	Moldova	Tunisia
Ecuador	Mongolia	Turkey
Egypt	Morocco	Uganda
El Salvador	Mozambique	Ukraine
Estonia	Myanmar	United Arab Emirates
Ethiopia	Namibia	United Kingdom
Finland	Netherlands	United States
France	New Zealand	Uruguay
Gabon	Nicaragua	República Bolivariana
Gambia, The	Niger	de Venezuela
Germany	Nigeria	Vietnam
Ghana	Norway	Yemen
Greece	Oman	Zambia
Guatemala	Pakistan	Zimbabwe

results in assessing the performance of the CEECs relative to their peers. However, the results from the global sample do a somewhat better job of matching actual and predicted growth rates. Following the discussion in the main text, explanatory variables are placed into two groups, those that are beyond the short-term control of policymakers and those that are potentially influenced by policy. The coefficient estimates are all correctly signed, are of plausible magnitudes, and are all significant with the exception of the relative price of investment in the global regression and the schooling variable in the advanced economy–emerging market subsample. The presence of the interaction term between institutional quality and initial income in the global regres-

sion implies that one cannot interpret the coefficient on (uninteracted) initial income as an indicator of conditional convergence; the convergence parameter in this regression is given by $\beta_0 + \beta_1 \cdot InstitutionalQuality$, where β_1 is the coefficient on the interaction term. The negative sign on β_1 implies that as institutional quality improves, convergence speeds increase, supporting the scatterplot in Figure 5.1.

The same regressions can be run using TFP growth and capital per capita growth as the dependent variables, enabling analysis of the channels through which these variables affect growth. These growth accounting regressions, whose results are described in the main text, can be found in Table A4.

Table A2. Growth Regressions with Core Controls, Using Different Country Samples

	Global		Developing Country		Emerging Market Country		Advanced and Emerging Market Country	
	Coefficient	t-statistic	Coefficient	t-statistic	Coefficient	t-statistic	Coefficient	t-statistic
Log of per capita GDP	−0.43	(2.40)	−0.16	(0.54)	−1.71	(6.10)	−1.71	(7.54)
Schooling	0.41	(3.22)	0.82	(2.45)	1.27	(5.87)	0.34	(2.99)
Population growth	−0.34	(5.34)	−0.28	(3.13)	−0.68	(4.55)	−0.68	(6.02)
Relative price of investment	−0.59	(3.80)	−0.30	(1.58)	−1.18	(3.79)	−1.09	(3.88)
Dummy, 2000–04	6.81	(4.47)	3.73	(1.65)	17.33	(6.65)	19.36	(8.87)
Dummy, 1995–99	6.12	(4.05)	2.93	(1.31)	16.24	(6.22)	18.87	(8.64)
Dummy, 1990–94	5.23	(3.38)	1.10	(0.48)	18.05	(6.89)	18.90	(8.60)
Dummy, 1985–89	5.81	(3.82)	1.85	(0.81)	17.49	(6.79)	19.22	(8.88)
Dummy, 1980–84	5.28	(3.42)	1.62	(0.69)	17.58	(6.79)	18.44	(8.48)
Dummy, 1975–79	6.55	(4.22)	3.09	(1.32)	19.20	(7.49)	19.54	(8.97)
Dummy, 1970–74	7.47	(4.90)	4.14	(1.80)	19.02	(7.56)	20.15	(9.40)
Dummy, 1965–69	7.41	(4.92)	3.68	(1.62)	19.19	(7.89)	20.32	(9.62)
Number of observations	740		356		218		384	

Source: IMF staff calculations.
Note: Dependent variable is five-year growth in real GDP per capita (PPP). Estimation method is seemingly unrelated regression.

Table A3. Growth Regression Estimates

	Global Sample		Advanced and Emerging Market Country Sample	
	Coefficient	t-statistic	Coefficient	t-statistic
Log of per capita GDP	1.36	(1.89)	−2.27	(6.34)
Population growth	−1.46	(8.94)	−1.27	(7.42)
Partner country growth	0.62	(3.39)	0.61	(3.24)
Relative price of investment goods	−0.22	(0.84)	−0.75	(2.41)
Schooling	0.45	(2.53)	0.20	(1.40)
Openness ratio	0.01	(3.01)	0.01	(3.85)
Government taxation ratio	−0.05	(2.17)	−0.02	(1.20)
Institutional quality	0.41	(4.07)	0.03	(1.88)
Institutional quality * log of per capita GDP	−0.04	(3.86)		
Dummy, 2000–04	−10.66	(1.69)	20.93	(6.74)
Dummy, 1995–99	−11.32	(1.80)	20.31	(6.50)
Dummy, 1990–94	−10.33	(1.65)	20.96	(6.72)
Dummy, 1985–89	−11.12	(1.78)	20.51	(6.50)
Number of observations	96, 84, 52, 56		58, 51, 41, 41	
R-squared	0.47, 0.02, 0.3, 0.37		0.58, −0.17, 0.36, 0.36	

Source: IMF staff calculations.
Note: The dependent variables are the growth rates of per capita GDP for the periods 2000–04, 1995–99, 1990–94, and 1985–89. Estimation method is seemingly unrelated regression.

Benchmark Models: Growth Predictions

Three general points emerge when comparing the benchmark model predictions and actual growth outcomes during the period 2000–04.

- Both models predict well. The relative rankings of the country groups are well matched: high-growth countries or regions have high predicted growths and vice versa. This can be seen in Figure A1, which reports the results for regional country groups and for the top

Table A4. Growth Accounting Regressions

	Global Sample						Advanced and Emerging Market Country Sample					
	GDP per capita		Capital per capita		TFP		GDP per capita		Capital per capita		TFP	
	Coefficient	t-statistics	Coefficient	t-statistics	Coefficient	t-statistics	Coefficient	t-statistics	Coefficient	t-statistics	Coefficient	t-statistics
Log of per capita GDP	1.36	(1.89)	1.08	(1.28)	1.55	(2.14)	-2.27	(6.34)	-2.39	(6.92)	-1.43	(4.55)
Population growth	-1.46	(8.94)	-0.87	(4.89)	-1.09	(7.87)	-1.27	(7.42)	-0.88	(4.87)	-0.99	(6.94)
Partner country growth	0.62	(3.39)	0.53	(2.72)	0.62	(3.78)	0.61	(3.24)	0.64	(3.31)	0.59	(3.44)
Schooling	0.45	(2.53)	0.13	(0.75)	0.46	(3.39)	-0.75	(2.41)	0.01	(0.08)	0.29	(2.31)
Relative price of investment	-0.22	(0.84)	-0.26	(1.02)	0.11	(0.58)	0.20	(1.40)	-0.94	(2.84)	-0.28	(1.08)
Openness ratio	0.009	(3.01)	0.009	(2.99)	0.009	(4.08)	0.010	(3.85)	0.009	(3.44)	0.009	(3.92)
Government taxation ratio	-0.05	(2.47)	-0.08	(3.92)	-0.02	(0.99)	-0.02	(1.20)	-0.05	(2.45)	-0.008	(0.46)
Institutional quality	0.41	(4.07)	0.39	(3.26)	0.32	(3.19)	0.03	(1.88)	0.08	(5.18)	-0.01	(0.75)
Institutions * log of per capita GDP	-0.04	(3.86)	-0.03	(2.60)	-0.04	(3.43)						
Dummy, 2000–04	-10.66	(1.69)	-11.21	(1.45)	-12.68	(1.92)	20.93	(6.74)	19.69	(6.44)	13.92	(5.21)
Dummy, 1995–99	-11.32	(1.80)	-11.28	(1.46)	-13.03	(1.97)	20.31	(6.50)	19.56	(6.38)	13.35	(4.97)
Dummy, 1990–94	-10.33	(1.65)	-10.54	(1.38)	-12.51	(1.91)	20.96	(6.72)	20.21	(6.59)	13.76	(5.13)
Dummy, 1985–89	-11.12	(1.78)	-11.54	(1.51)	-12.98	(1.98)	20.51	(6.50)	18.82	(6.09)	13.63	(5.01)
Number of observations	288		255		255		191		187		187	

Source: IMF staff calculations.

Figure A1. Emerging Market Countries: Actual and Predicted Per Capita GDP Growth, 2000–04
(In percent, PPP, annual average)

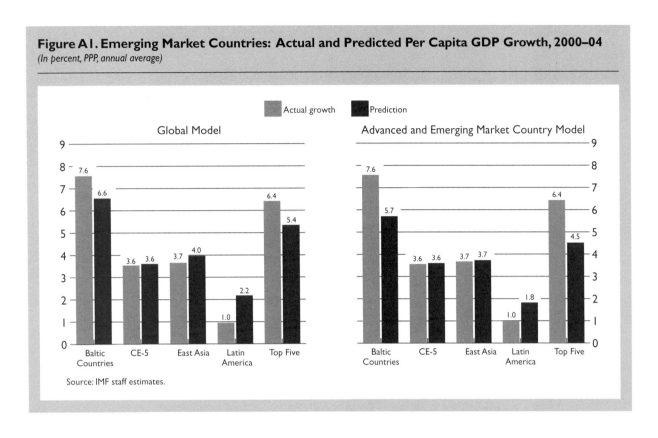

Source: IMF staff estimates.

Figure A2. CEECs: Actual and Predicted Per Capita GDP Growth, 2000–04
(In percent, PPP, annual average)

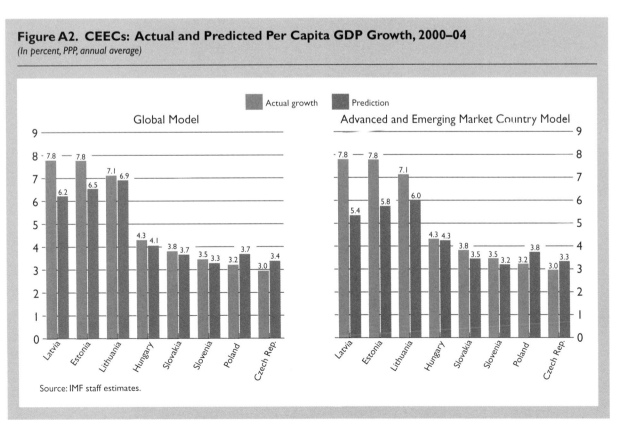

Source: IMF staff estimates.

five emerging market performers excluding the Baltics.

- Predictions are particularly close in absolute, or cardinal, terms in the mid-ranges of growth rates and diverge at the two extreme ends. At the high end, the Baltics and the top five performers are predicted to have lower growth rates than they actually achieved. In contrast, Latin America, which achieved particular low average per capita growth during this period should, the models say, have achieved higher growth. Thus, it appears as if extreme growth rates are the outcomes of special circumstances not easily captured by such growth models. Countries with very rapid growth already have the potential to grow fast, as implied by their high predicted growth rates, but, in addition, are positioned to benefit from positive surprises. In contrast, countries with lower growth potential are the ones most hurt by negative growth surprises.

- Finally, while both models do well, the "global" model outperforms slightly with somewhat better predictions. While it is difficult to be precise in assessing the source of this difference, there is probably one substantive reason and another technical reason. Substantively, the global model allows for differing speeds of convergence. While the speeds of conditional convergence in emerging market countries and advanced economies are close, it appears that advanced countries, with their better institutions, may converge slightly faster. We are not able to pick up that nuance in the smaller sample. This leads to the second technical reason for the difference. In the smaller sample, the variation in explanatory variables is smaller, making it harder to achieve estimates with great precision.

The models are almost spot-on in predicting the average growth rates in the CE-5, but underpredict growth in the Baltics (Figure A2). For the CE-5, both the actual and predicted growth rates are around $3\frac{1}{2}$ percent a year. Once again, the predicted ranks for country growth rates line up with the actual performance and in no case is the difference between actual and predicted growth rates more than $\frac{1}{2}$ percentage point. With respect to the Baltics, which achieved an annual average growth rate of $7\frac{1}{2}$ percent over this period, the global model predicts a $6\frac{1}{2}$ percent growth rate and the advanced economy–emerging market model predicts a little over $5\frac{1}{2}$ percent. Once again, looking at the individual countries, growth rates are underpredicted, but less so by the global model, which comes close to matching Lithuania's actual achievement.

Decomposition of Growth Differences

The growth regressions can provide useful decompositions of the importance of various factors in explaining differences in growth rates across regions or countries (Tables A5 and A6). The decomposition of growth predictions when no interaction terms are present is straightforward: it is given by (suppressing subscripts):

$$\hat{y} - \hat{y}^R = \beta'(X - X^R),$$

where the superscript R denotes the reference country.

In the benchmark model, the effects of the interaction between initial income per capita and institutional quality needs to be reallocated into the part that is due to differences in initial income and the part that is due to differences in institutional quality. This is done as follows. Predicted growth for a country/region and the reference country/region are given by

$$\hat{y}_t = \beta_0 y_{t-1} + \beta_1 I_{t-1} + \beta_2 y_{t-1} I_{t-1} + \beta'X_{t-1}$$

$$\hat{y}_t^R = \beta_0 y_{t-1}^R + \beta_1 I_{t-1}^R + \beta_2 y_{t-1}^R I_{t-1}^R + \beta'X_{t-1}^R.$$

Subtracting the second equation from the first gives

$$\hat{y}_t - \hat{y}_t^R = \beta_0(y_{t-1} - y_{t-1}^R) + \beta_1(I_{t-1} - I_{t-1}^R)$$
$$+ \beta'(X_{t-1} - X_{t-1}^R) + \beta_2(y_{t-1} I_{t-1} - y_{t-1}^R I_{t-1}^R).$$

To reallocate the second term to differences in initial income and institutional quality, add and subtract $\beta_2 I_{t-1} y_{t-1}^R$ and rearrange this with the last term above to get:

$$\hat{y}_t - \hat{y}_t^R = \beta_0(y_{t-1} - y_{t-1}^R) + \beta_1(I_{t-1} - I_{t-1}^R) + \beta'(X_{t-1} - X_{t-1}^R)$$
$$+ \beta_2(y_{t-1} I_{t-1} - y_{t-1}^R I_{t-1}^R) + \beta_2 I_{t-1} y_{t-1}^R - \beta_2 I_{t-1} y_{t-1}^R$$
$$= \beta_0(y_{t-1} - y_{t-1}^R) + \beta_1(I_{t-1} - I_{t-1}^R) + \beta'(X_{t-1} - X_{t-1}^R)$$
$$+ \beta_2 I_{t-1}(y_{t-1} - y_{t-1}^R) + \beta_2 y_{t-1}^R(I_{t-1} - I_{t-1}^R).$$

Finally, combine terms to get

$$\hat{y}_t - \hat{y}_t^R = (\beta_0 + \beta_2 I_{t-1})(y_{t-1} - y_{t-1}^R) + (\beta_1 + \beta_2 y_{t-1}^R)$$
$$(I_{t-1} - I_{t-1}^R) + \beta'(X_{t-1} - X_{t-1}^R).$$

Note that one can also perform the decomposition by adding and subtracting $\beta_2 I_{t-1}^R y_{t-1}$, which would give a similar formula:

$$\hat{y}_t - \hat{y}_t^R = (\beta_0 + \beta_2 I_{t-1}^R)(y_{t-1} - y_{t-1}^R) + (\beta_1 + \beta_2 y_{t-1})(I_{t-1} - I_{t-1}^R)$$
$$+ \beta'(X_{t-1} - X_{t-1}^R).$$

This decomposition allocates the cross term, $\beta_2(y_{t-1} - y_{t-1}^R)(I_{t-1} - I_{t-1}^R)$, to differences due to initial income, while

Table A5. CE-5: Decomposition of Growth Differences

	East Asia		Latin America		Baltic countries		Top five emerging market countries		OECD countries	
	\<div\>CE-5 Performance (2000–04) Relative to\</div\>									
	Global regression	Advanced and emerging market country regression	Global regression	Advanced and emerging market country regression	Global regression	Advanced and emerging market country regression	Global regression	Advanced and emerging market country regression	Global regression	Advanced and emerging market country regression
Difference in GDP per capita growth to be explained	–0.1		2.7		–4.0		–2.9		1.4	
Difference explained by "exogenous" variables										
Log of per capita GDP	–0.45	–0.52	–1.19	–1.49	–0.79	–0.93	–1.14	–1.44	1.06	1.14
Population growth	1.86	1.62	2.28	1.98	–1.00	–0.87	0.24	0.21	0.90	0.78
Partner country growth	–0.87	–0.86	–0.18	–0.18	–0.82	–0.80	–0.63	–0.61	–0.21	–0.20
Subtotal	0.54	0.24	0.90	0.31	–2.61	–2.59	–1.53	–1.85	1.76	1.72
Difference explained by "policy-influenced" variables										
Schooling	–0.20	–0.09	0.40	0.18	–0.27	–0.12	–0.29	–0.13	–0.55	–0.24
Relative price of investment	–0.01	–0.02	0.17	0.58	0.15	0.52	0.10	0.34	–0.05	–0.16
Openness	–0.32	–0.34	0.19	0.20	–0.09	–0.10	0.33	0.36	0.22	0.24
Institutional quality	0.02	0.10	0.14	0.31	0.03	0.12	0.15	0.34	0.04	–0.11
Tax revenue/GDP	–0.57	–0.25	–0.44	–0.20	–0.18	–0.08	–0.53	–0.24	0.03	0.01
Subtotal	–1.08	–0.60	0.45	1.07	–0.35	0.35	–0.24	0.67	–0.30	–0.26
Total explained difference	–0.54	–0.36	1.35	1.38	–2.96	–2.25	–1.77	–1.17	1.45	1.47

Source: IMF staff calculations.

Table A6. Baltic Countries: Decomposition of Growth Differences

	Baltic Countries' Performance (2000–04) Relative to									
	East Asia		Latin America		CE-5		Top five emerging market countries		OECD countries	
	3.9		6.7		4.0		1.2		5.4	
Difference in GDP per capita growth to be explained	Global regression	Advanced and emerging market country regression	Global regression	Advanced and emerging market country regression	Global regression	Advanced and emerging market country regression	Global regression	Advanced and emerging market country regression	Global regression	Advanced and emerging market country regression
Difference explained by "exogenous" variables										
Log of per capita GDP	0.33	0.40	−0.43	−0.57	0.79	0.93	−0.39	−0.51	1.84	2.07
Population growth	2.86	2.48	3.27	2.84	1.00	0.87	1.24	1.07	1.90	1.65
Partner country growth	−0.05	−0.05	0.64	0.63	0.82	0.80	0.19	0.19	0.61	0.60
Subtotal	3.14	2.83	3.48	2.90	2.61	2.59	1.04	0.75	4.36	4.32
Difference explained by "policy-influenced" variables										
Schooling	0.07	0.03	0.67	0.29	0.27	0.12	−0.02	−0.01	−0.28	−0.12
Relative price of investment	−0.15	−0.54	0.02	0.06	−0.15	−0.52	−0.05	−0.18	−0.19	−0.68
Openness	−0.23	−0.24	0.28	0.30	0.09	0.10	0.42	0.45	0.31	0.33
Institutional quality	−0.01	−0.02	0.14	0.19	−0.03	−0.12	0.16	0.22	0.02	−0.23
Tax revenue/GDP	−0.39	−0.17	−0.27	−0.12	0.18	0.08	−0.36	−0.16	0.20	0.09
Subtotal	−0.72	−0.95	0.84	0.72	0.35	−0.35	0.15	0.33	0.06	−0.61
Total explained difference	2.42	1.89	4.32	3.62	2.96	2.25	1.20	1.07	4.42	3.71

Source: IMF staff calculations.

the first decomposition allocates it to differences due to institutional quality. Since the cross-term is due to both types of differences, this choice is arbitrary.

A final alternative would be to "split the difference" and attribute equal parts of the cross term to initial income differences and institutional quality differences:

$$\hat{y}_t - \hat{y}_t^R = (\beta_0 + \beta_2 (I_{t-1} + I_{t-1}^R)/2)(y_{t-1} - y_{t-1}^R)$$
$$+ (\beta_1 + \beta_2 (y_{t-1} + y_{t-1}^R)/2)(I_{t-1} - I_{t-1}^R)$$
$$+ \beta'(X_{t-1} - X_{t-1}^R).$$

This also has the advantage of being symmetric, so that a decomposition of $\hat{y}_t^1 - \hat{y}_t^2$ (that is, where country/region 2 is used as the reference) will provide the same breakdown as that for $\hat{y}_t^2 - \hat{y}_t^1$ (where country/region 1 is used as the reference). This is the decomposition formula used here.

Modeling Financial Integration and Growth in the EU

This section provides a brief description of the model of financial integration and growth in the EU, which was used in Section VI of the main text. Within this group of countries there is a clear link between growth and current account deficits, with higher growth being associated with larger current account deficits, both over short one-year horizons and over longer periods (Figure A3). The best-fit line suggests that an increase in the current account deficit of 2 percentage points of GDP is associated with a 1–1.4 percentage point increase in GDP growth. Deviations from the best-fit line are also informative, as they show that some countries are growing rapidly at present without incurring significant external liabilities, while others could be expected to grow faster given the level of the current account (or conversely, that they should have a lower current account deficit given their present growth rates).

Theoretical models suggest, however, that this relationship is bidirectional and complex. Current accounts are affected by the level of per capita income, with lower levels of per capita income associated with greater external borrowing. In addition, Blanchard and Giavazzi (2002) note that the growth rate of income can also affect the current account, as it is an indicator of future growth prospects, and also captures cyclical effects of output movements on the current account. But current account deficits also affect growth, in two ways. Most obviously, external borrowing removes constraints on investment and consumption. An additional effect is suggested by open-economy versions of the neoclassical growth model, as elaborated, for

example, by Barro and Sala-i-Martin (2004). In an open economy, if factors are fully mobile and the technology across countries does not differ, factor returns should equalize almost instantaneously, achieving income convergence. If, however, some forms of capital (e.g., human capital) provide unacceptable security for loans, then the extent of foreign debt will be limited by quantity of physical capital that can serve as collateral. In such a model, Barro and Sala-i-Martin write, "the opportunity to borrow on the world credit market . . . will turn out to affect the *speed of convergence*" (p. 105). Empirically, this suggests that the coefficient on per capita income in standard growth regressions may itself be influenced by the current account, as explained below.

The empirical specification of the above model consists of two simultaneous equations for the current account and for growth. In equation (1), growth in per capita income in country i in year t, Δy_{it}, depends on lagged income relative to the steady-state income level, $(y_{it-1} - y_{t-1}^*)$. The steady-state income level, y_t^*, is allowed to change over time, but is assumed to be the same for all the countries in the sample. If poor countries grow faster as they converge to income levels of their richer neighbors, then the coefficient on lagged relative income should be negative. Here, this "speed of convergence" coefficient consists of two parts: a part that is influenced by the current account, $\alpha_2 ca_{it-1}$, and an independent part, α_{1t}. If current account deficits $(ca_{it} < 0)$ accelerate income convergence, then the coefficient α_2 should be positive. The specification also allows for the possibility that the current account influences actual growth directly, and this effect is captured by the terms $\alpha_3 ca_{it-1}$. In addition, growth is allowed to be influenced by standard neoclassical growth controls, that is, schooling and population growth, that are denoted by matrix $Z_{1,it}$. The growth equation is thus

$$\Delta y_{it} = x + (\alpha_{1t} + \alpha_2 ca_{it-1})(y_{it-1} - y_{t-1}^*)$$
$$+ \alpha_3 ca_{it-1} + \alpha_4 Z_{1,it}, \qquad (1)$$

where x is the steady-state growth rate, often associated with the rate of technological progress in the literature. Finally, actual growth is allowed to be influenced by cyclical factors that may change from year to year. For this reason, equation (1) is augmented by a year dummy, D_t, which equals one in year t and zero otherwise. The equation can be rewritten as

$$\Delta y_{it} = \alpha_{0t} + (\alpha_{1t} + \alpha_2 ca_{it-1})y_{it-1} + \alpha_3 ca_{it-1}$$
$$+ \alpha_4 Z_{1,it} + (v_{1i} + \varepsilon_{1it}), \qquad (2)$$

where the term $\alpha_{0t} = x - \alpha_{1t} y_{t-1}^* + \alpha_5 D_t$, and $(v_{1i} + \varepsilon_{1it})$ represents a mean-zero composite error term.

Figure A3. Current Account Balances and GDP Growth in the European Union, 2000–04

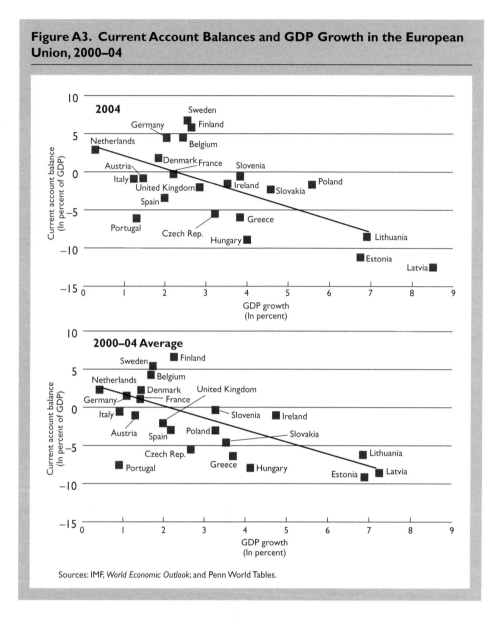

Sources: IMF, *World Economic Outlook*; and Penn World Tables.

Equation (3) describes the dynamics of the current account. The current-account-to-GDP ratio in country i in year t, ca_{it}, depends on the current level of income, y_{it}, on current growth, Δy_{it}, and on the dependency ratio, denoted by Z_2. Other things equal, a country with a relatively high dependency ratio is expected to save less.

$$ca_{it} = \beta_{1t}(y_{it}-y_t^*)+\beta_{2t}\Delta y_{it}+\beta_3 Z_{2,it}. \qquad (3)$$

The specification is largely standard, except that the effect of income per capita on the current account is allowed to vary over time, following Blanchard and Giavazzi (2002). If the process of increasing financial integration in Europe enabled poor countries to borrow more and rich countries to lend more, then one would expect the coefficient on relative income, β_{1t} to increase over time. As in standard specifications, current growth also enters the equation, both as a predictor of future income and in order to capture cyclical effects of output movements on the current account. The effect of growth on the current account is also allowed to vary over time. Finally, as in the growth equation, the equation has a common time effect, captured by the year dummy, D_t. The equation can thus be rewritten as:

$$ca_{it} = \beta_{0t}+\beta_{1t}y_{it}+\beta_{2t}\Delta y_{it}+\beta_3 Z_{2,it}+(v_{2i}+\varepsilon_{2it}), \qquad (4)$$

where the term $\beta_{0t}=-\beta_{1t}y_t^*+\beta_4 D_t$, and $(v_{2i}+\varepsilon_{2it})$ represents a mean-zero composite error term.

Table A7. Growth and Current Account Deficit Regressions

	Growth Equation	Current Account Deficit Equation
Log of per capita GDP[1]	−4.76	−10.52
	[4.17]***	[4.86]***
Schooling	0.25	
	[2.59]***	
Population growth	−0.06	
	[0.22]	
Current account deficit	3.68	
	[3.25]***	
Log of per capita GDP * CA deficit	−0.39	
	[3.31]***	
Old-age dependency ratio		0.08
		[2.02]**
Growth of per capita GDP[1]		0.12
		[0.51]
Number of observations	503	503
R-squared	0.49	0.52

Source: IMF staff calculations.

Note: For ease of exposition, the table presents results in terms of the current account deficit rather than the current account balance. Absolute value of z-statistics in brackets. *, **, and *** indicate significance at 10 percent, 5 percent, and 1 percent levels, respectively.

[1]The coefficients on income and on growth are time-varying. For these variables, the table shows the parameter estimates for 2004.

The estimation method used is three-stage least squares, a standard technique for the estimation of simultaneous equations in the panel data context. This method, first proposed by Zellner and Theil (1962), permits the estimation of a system of equations, where some of the explanatory variables are endogenous. Here, both the current account and growth are explanatory variables and are endogenous. The three-stage least-squares procedure uses an instrumental variable approach to produce consistent estimates and generalized least squares to account for the correlation structure in the disturbances across the equations. For further discussion of the three-stage least-squares approach to estimation, see, for instance, Greene (2003, pp. 405–407). Table A7 presents the estimation results based on EU-25 data from 1975 to 2004.

Once the parameters are estimated, the model can be used to generate predicted values of the current account and growth, along with 95 confidence intervals. These benchmark values can be compared to actual outcomes to assess the performance of growth and the current account. The (in-sample) predicted values are obtained using the equations:

$$\Delta \ddot{y}_{it} = \hat{\alpha}_{0t} + (\hat{\alpha}_{1t} + \hat{\alpha}_4 \, ca_{it-1}) y_{it-1} + \hat{\alpha}_2 ca_{it-1} + \hat{\alpha}_3 Z_{1,it} \quad (5)$$

$$\hat{ca}_{it} = \hat{\beta}_{0t} + \hat{\beta}_{1t} y_{it} + \hat{\beta}_{2t} \Delta y_{it} + \hat{\beta}_3 Z_{2,it}, \quad (6)$$

where the "^" superscripts denote estimates. For each period t, the matrix of prediction standard errors is denoted by s_t. The standard errors are computed using the following formula:

$$s_t = \sqrt{x_t V x_t'}, \quad (7)$$

where x_t is the matrix of right-hand-side variables up to and including period t, and V is the estimated variance covariance matrix of the parameter estimates. Standard error bands around the predicted values can then be computed using a band of ±1.96 times the prediction standard errors. Estimates of the key parameters as well as the predicted current accounts and growth rates can be found in Table A7, the table in Box 6.1, and Figures 6.3 and 6.4. Further estimation details, as well as robustness checks, can be found in Abiad and Leigh (2005).

Data Description

The set of countries covered by the study was determined by the availability of key variables; small countries (with population less than one million) were also excluded. The global sample of 125 countries that are in the data set are listed in Table A1. Within this global sample, we define a group of emerging market countries

Table A8. Emerging Market Economies

Argentina	Israel	Russia
Brazil	Jordan	Singapore
Bulgaria	Korea	Slovakia
Chile	Latvia	Slovenia
China	Lebanon	South Africa
Colombia	Lithuania	Sri Lanka
Croatia	Malaysia	Taiwan Province
Czech Rep.	Mexico	of China
Egypt	Morocco	Thailand
Estonia	Pakistan	Turkey
Hong Kong SAR	Peru	República
Hungary	Philippines	Bolivariana de
India	Poland	Venezuela
Indonesia	Romania	

as those covered by the Morgan Stanley Capital International Emerging Markets index; in addition, all of the EU's new member states and accession candidates are treated as emerging market countries. The countries included in the emerging market country sample are listed in Table A8. Finally, we identify a subsample of 21 advanced economies, defined as the set of OECD countries that are not in the emerging market country subsample. Data were collected in the early part of 2005 and so may not reflect more recent revisions.

Income levels and growth rates are chain-weighted real GDP per capita in PPP terms (*rgdpch*) from Penn World Tables (PWT) Version 6.1 (http://pwt.econ.upenn.edu/). As these data end in 2000 and are sparse for the Baltic countries, we supplement and extend this using growth rates from the World Bank's *World Development Indicators* (*WDI*) or the IMF's *World Economic Outlook* (*WEO*). To analyze the impact of physical capital accumulation we use the relative price of investment, which was found by SDM(2004) to be more robust than investment share as a growth determinant, and which is also less subject to endogeneity. Relative price of investment is calculated as the ratio of

the investment price deflator to the GDP deflator, both of which are also taken from PWT. Data for the growth accounting regressions were taken from Bosworth and Collins (2003).

Data on schooling are taken from the Barro-Lee educational attainment data set (http://post.economics.harvard.edu/faculty/barro/data.html), and are defined as the average years of secondary and higher education in the population. For countries not covered by the Barro-Lee data set, we regress their data on secondary and tertiary enrollment rates from the *WDI* and use predicted values from that regression. Population growth is from the *WDI*, supplemented when missing with PWT data.

Openness is the sum of exports and imports divided by GDP, defined as the variable *openc* in PWT. This was supplemented by *WEO* data when missing. Tax revenue to GDP is taken from several sources, including the OECD database, the IMF's *Government Finance Statistics*, and the *WDI*. Partner country growth is from the Global Economic Environment of the *WEO*, and is calculated as the average of growth in partner countries, weighted by their shares in total exports. The dependency ratio is taken from the *WDI*, and is defined as the share of the population that is either younger than 15 years or older than 64 years divided by the share of the population that is between the ages of 15 and 64.

Finally, our measure of institutional quality is taken from the *International Country Risk Guide*, compiled by the private consultancy firm Political Risk Services. This data set covers 143 countries, from 1984 to the present. First used by Keefer and Knack (1997), it has become a standard measure of institutional quality in the literature, as it has the advantage of both cross-sectional breadth and long-time coverage. The composite index is an aggregation of various subcomponents that measure factors such as government stability, democratic accountability, law and order, quality of bureaucracy, and corruption in government. To ensure comparability among countries and over time, points are assigned based on preset questions for each risk subcomponent.

References

Abiad, Abdul, and Daniel Leigh, 2005, "Growth and Current Account Performance: Results from a Cross-Country Model," in *Hungary: Selected Issues*, IMF Country Report No. 05/215 (Washington: International Monetary Fund).

Abiad, Abdul, and Ashoka Mody, 2005, "Financial Reform: What Shakes It? What Shapes It?" *American Economic Review*, Vol. 95 (March), pp. 66–88.

Acemoglu, Daron, Simon Johnson, and James A. Robinson, 2001, "The Colonial Origins of Comparative Development: An Empirical Investigation," *American Economic Review*, Vol. 91 (December), pp. 1369–1401.

Adam, Christopher S., and David L. Bevan, 2005, "Fiscal Deficits and Growth in Developing Countries," *Journal of Public Economics*, Vol. 89 (April), pp. 571–97.

Aghion, Philippe, and Peter Howitt, 2005, "Appropriate Growth Policy: A Unifying Framework," 2005 Joseph Schumpeter Lecture, delivered at the Twentieth Annual Congress of the European Economic Association, August 25.

Arora, Vivek B., and Athanasios Vamvakidis, 2005, "How Much Do Trading Partners Matter for Economic Growth?" *IMF Staff Papers*, Vol. 52 (No. 1), pp. 24–40.

Barro, Robert J., and Xavier Sala-i-Martin, 2004, *Economic Growth*, 2nd ed. (Cambridge, Massachusetts: MIT Press).

Barth, James R., Gerard Caprio, and Ross Levine, 2006, *Rethinking Bank Regulation: Till Angels Govern* (Cambridge, England: Cambridge University Press).

Beck, Thorsten, Ross Levine, and Norman Loayza, 2000, "Finance and the Sources of Growth," *Journal of Financial Economics*, Vol. 58 (No. 1–2), pp. 261–300.

Blanchard, Olivier, and Francesco Giavazzi, 2002, "Current Account Deficits in the Euro Area: The End of the Feldstein-Horioka Puzzle?" *Brookings Papers on Economic Activity: 2*, pp. 147–209.

Bosworth, Barry P., and Susan M. Collins, 2003, "The Empirics of Growth: An Update," *Brookings Papers on Economic Activity: 2*, pp. 113–206.

Burnside, Craig, and David Dollar, 2000, "Aid, Policies, and Growth," *American Economic Review*, Vol. 90 (September), pp. 847–68.

Campos, Nauro F., and Abrizio Coricelli, 2002, "Growth in Transition: What We Know, What We Don't, and What We Should," *Journal of Economic Literature*, Vol. 40, No. 3, pp. 793–836.

Caselli, Francesco, and Silvana Tenreyro, 2005, "Is Poland the Next Spain?" NBER Working Paper No. 11045 (Cambridge, Massachusetts: National Bureau of Economic Research).

Choueiri, Nada, 2005, "The Labor Market in Poland," in *Republic of Poland: Selected Issues*, IMF Country Report No. 05/264 (Washington: International Monetary Fund).

Crafts, Nicholas, and Kai Kaiser, 2004, "Long-Term Growth Prospects in Transition Economies: A Reappraisal," *Structural Change and Economic Dynamics*, Vol. 15, Issue 1, pp. 101–18.

Doyle, Peter, Louis Kuijs, and Guorong Jiang, 2001, "Real Convergence to EU Income Levels: Central Europe from 1990 to the Long Term," IMF Working Paper No. 01/146 (Washington: International Monetary Fund).

Easterly, William, 2005, "National Policies and Economic Growth: A Reappraisal," in *Handbook of Economic Growth*, Vol. 1, ed. by Philippe Aghion and Steven N. Durlauf (Amsterdam; Boston: Elsevier, North-Holland).

Edwards, Sebastian, 2003, "Public Sector Deficits, Macroeconomic Stability, and Economic Performance," in *Reforming India's External, Financial, and Fiscal Policies*, ed. by Anne O. Krueger and Sajjid Z. Chinoy (Stanford, California: Stanford University Press).

Estevão, Marcello, 2003, "Structural and Cyclical Labor Market Changes in Poland," in *Republic of Poland: Selected Issues*, IMF Country Report No. 03/188 (Washington: International Monetary Fund).

European Bank for Reconstruction and Development (EBRD), 2004, *Transition Report* (London).

Faruqee, Hamid, 2004, "Measuring the Trade Effects of EMU," IMF Working Paper No. 04/154 (Washington: International Monetary Fund).

Fatás, A., and I. Mihov, 2003, "The Case for Restricting Fiscal Policy Discretion," *Quarterly Journal of Economics*, Vol. 118 (No. 4), pp. 1419–47.

Fischer, Stanley, Ratna Sahay, and Carlos Végh, 1996, "Stabilization and Growth in Transition Economies: The Early Experience," *Journal of Economic Perspectives*, Vol. 10 (No. 2), pp. 45–66.

Gallup, John Luke, Jeffrey D. Sachs, and Andrew D. Mellinger, 1999, "Geography and Economic Development," *International Regional Science Review*, Vol. 22 (No. 2), pp. 179–232.

Ghosh, Atish R., Anne-Marie Gulde, and Holger C. Wolf, 2002, *Exchange Rate Regimes: Choices and Consequences* (Cambridge, Massachusetts: MIT Press).

Glaeser, Edward L., and others, 2004, "Do Institutions Cause Growth?" *Journal of Economic Growth*, Vol. 9 (No. 3), pp. 271–303.

Gomes, Tamara, and others, 2004, "The Euro and Trade: Is There a Positive Effect?" (unpublished; Ottawa: Bank of Canada).

Greene, William, 2003, *Econometric Analysis*, 5th ed. (Upper Saddle River, New Jersey: Prentice Hall).

Harberger, Arnold C., 2003, "Parking the Deficit: The Uncertain Link Between Fiscal Deficits and Inflation-Cum-Devaluation," in *Reforming India's External, Financial, and Fiscal Policies*, ed. by Anne O. Krueger and Sajjid Z. Chinoy (Stanford, California: Stanford University Press).

Havrylyshyn, Oleh, and Ron van Rooden, 2000, "Institutions Matter in Transition, But So Do Policies," IMF Working Paper No. 00/70 (Washington: International Monetary Fund).

Husain, Aasim M., Ashoka Mody, and Kenneth S. Rogoff, 2005, "Exchange Rate Durability and Performance in Developing Versus Advanced Economies," *Journal of Monetary Economics*, Vol. 52 (January), pp. 35–64.

International Monetary Fund (IMF), 2003, "Growth and Institutions," *World Economic Outlook*, April, World Economic and Financial Surveys (Washington: International Monetary Fund).

Kátay, Gábor, and Zoltán Wolf, 2006, "Measuring Productivity at the Firm Level" (unpublished; Budapest: National Bank of Hungary).

Kaufmann, Daniel, Aart Kraay, and Massimi Mastruzzi, 2005, *Governance Matters IV: Governance Indicators for 1996–2004*, Policy Research Working Paper No. 3630 (Washington: World Bank).

Keane, Michael P., and Eswar S. Prasad, 2000, "Inequality, Transfers and Growth: New Evidence from the Economic Transition in Poland," IMF Working Paper No. 00/117 (Washington: International Monetary Fund).

Keefer, Philip, and Stephen Knack, 1997, "Why Don't Poor Countries Catch Up? A Cross-National Test of an Institutional Explanation," *Economic Inquiry*, Vol. 35 (July), pp. 590–602.

Levine, Ross, 1997, "Financial Development and Economic Growth: Views and Agenda," *Journal of Economic Literature*, Vol. 35 (June), pp. 688–726.

———, Norman Loayza, and Thorsten Beck, 2000, "Financial Intermediation and Growth: Causality and Causes," *Journal of Monetary Economics*, Vol. 46 (August), pp. 31–77.

Levine, Ross, and David Renelt, 1992, "A Sensitivity Analysis of Cross-Country Growth Regressions," *American Economic Review*, Vol. 82 (September), pp. 942–63.

Lipschitz, Leslie, Timothy Lane, and Alex Mourmouras, 2002, "Capital Flows to Transition Economies: Master or Servant?" IMF Working Paper No. 02/11 (Washington: International Monetary Fund).

———, 2005, "Real Convergence, Capital Flows, and Monetary Policy: Notes on the European Transition Countries," in *Euro Adoption in Central and Eastern Europe: Opportunities and Challenges*, ed. by Susan Schadler (Washington: International Monetary Fund).

Lucas, Robert E., 1990, "Why Doesn't Capital Flow from Rich to Poor Countries?" *American Economic Review, Papers and Proceedings*, Vol. 80 (May), pp. 92–96.

Mody, Ashoka, and Antu Panini Murshid, 2005, "Growing Up with Capital Flows," *Journal of International Economics*, Vol. 65 (No. 1), pp. 249–66.

Organization for Economic Cooperation and Development (OECD), 2004, "Enhancing Income Convergence in Central Europe after EU Accession," Chap. 7 in *OECD Economic Outlook*, No. 75 (Paris).

Piatkowski, Marcin, 2006, "Can ICT Make a Difference?" *Information Technologies and International Development*, Vol. 3, No. 1 (Fall), forthcoming.

Rajan, Raghuram, and Luigi Zingales, 2003, *Saving Capitalism from the Capitalists* (New York: Crown Business).

Rogoff, Kenneth S., and others, 2004, *Evolution and Performance of Exchange Rate Regimes*, IMF Occasional Paper No. 229 (Washington: International Monetary Fund).

Sachs, Jeffrey D., and Andrew M. Warner, 1995, "Economic Reform and the Process of Economic Integration," *Brookings Papers on Economic Activity: 1*, pp. 1–95.

Sala-i-Martin, Xavier, Gernot Doppelhofer, and Ronald I. Miller, 2004, "Determinants of Long-Term Growth: A Bayesian Averaging of Classical Estimates (BACE) Approach," *American Economic Review*, Vol. 94 (September), pp. 813–35.

Schadler, Susan, and others, 2005, *Adopting the Euro in Central Europe: Challenges of the Next Step in European Integration*, IMF Occasional Paper No. 234 (Washington: International Monetary Fund).

Schiff, Jerald, and others, 2006, *Labor Market Performance in Transition: The Experience of Central and Eastern European Countries*, IMF Occasional Paper No. 248 (Washington: International Monetary Fund).

World Bank, 2005, *Economic Growth in the 1990s: Learning from a Decade of Reform* (Washington).

Zellner, Arnold, and H. Theil, 1962, "Three-Stage Least Squares: Simultaneous Estimation of Simultaneous Equations," *Econometrica*, Vol. 30 (January), pp. 54–78.

Concluding Remarks by the Acting Chair

Growth in the Central and Eastern European Countries of the European Union

Executive Board Seminar, February 27, 2006

Today's Board seminar has been a welcome opportunity for Directors to discuss the challenges facing the Central and Eastern European countries (CEECs) of the European Union (EU) as they raise living standards to Western European levels. Directors welcomed the staff's comprehensive analysis of the CEECs' recent growth performance, the policies required to support rapid catch-up, and the vulnerabilities that will need to be monitored as convergence proceeds. They also made a number of useful suggestions on how the analysis of these issues can be deepened going forward, including with some case studies, and looked forward to similar regional surveillance reviews in the future.

Directors recognized the difficulty in disentangling the unique forces that shaped the CEECs' growth over the past 15 years, including the steep post-transition drop in output, the macroeconomic and institutional reforms related to EU accession, and the benign global conditions in the more recent period. While the CEECs' per capita output growth in the past five years has put them in the upper half of the emerging market comparator group—with the Baltics among the top five performers—Directors cautioned that the continuation of these rapid growth rates cannot be taken for granted.

Directors noted important differences in the pattern of growth in the CEECs vis-à-vis other emerging markets, particularly the lack of employment growth, and the heavy contribution of total factor productivity (TFP) gains. They acknowledged that the convergence experience of other EU members, such as Greece, Ireland, Portugal, and Spain, demonstrates the viability of sustained periods of high productivity growth. Nevertheless, they pointed out that the CEECs' recent TFP growth may have been heavily influenced by the elimination of the inefficiencies of central planning—implying the possibility of some trailing off in the absence of strong efforts to improve the business environment.

Directors emphasized that prospects for the CEECs will depend on how well they do in establishing macroeconomic and structural conditions conducive to sustained growth, which is expected to be based on greater labor use and higher investment rates. They welcomed staff's use of empirical growth models to shed light on the key environmental and policy characteristics that will shape the CEECs' growth prospects. Directors noted that certain environmental features—including initial income gaps, population growth and aging, and historical trade relationships—as well as conditions more subject to policy influence play important roles in supporting growth. Among the latter, our discussion highlighted, in particular, the quality of legal and economic institutions, size of government, real cost of investment, educational attainment and labor market performance, openness to trade, and inflation. While Directors were encouraged that the CEECs do reasonably well in meeting these conditions, they also noted that differences tend to favor growth in the Baltics over the CE-5, reinforcing other indications that a two-speed catch-up—rapid for the Baltics, more moderate for the CE-5—may be emerging.

Directors agreed that the process of European integration will play a critical role in supporting a rapid catch-up in the CEECs. Substantial transfers from the European Union to the new member states are one obvious benefit, but potentially more important will be the benefits from closer institutional, trade, and financial integration with Western Europe. In this regard, Directors were encouraged by indications that thus far foreign savings have contributed significantly and appropriately to growth in most CEECs, and that the even large current account deficits of some countries have been in line with their growth rates.

Directors observed, however, that alongside the scope for accelerating the convergence process are the risks that increased reliance on foreign savings will generate significant vulnerabilities in the CEECs. They noted that large current account deficits are a potential source of increased indebtedness. The use of foreign savings, therefore, needs to be watched closely, and the composition of current account deficits—including the extent to which they are caused by reinvested earnings on foreign direct investment—deserves careful assessment. The use of foreign savings has also stimulated rapid credit growth both for businesses and, especially for households that have had little access to credit, growing confidence in the future means sizable borrowing to smooth consumption. In this regard, Directors cautioned that, especially in the Baltics and Hungary, various combinations of high external debt ratios, rapid credit growth (with a sizable share in foreign currency), and, in the Baltics, low reserve coverage of short-term debt need to be monitored carefully. For the immediate future, Directors were reassured that a number of factors—high reserves in the CE-5, strong fiscal positions in the Baltics, satisfactory competitiveness, relatively high standards of transparency, and well-supervised and predominantly foreign-owned banks—help mitigate these vulnerabilities.

Against this backdrop, our discussion identified a number of policy priorities for CEEC governments. Among them, the need to establish cushions against shocks; to contribute to domestic savings appropriately through sizable fiscal surpluses when catch-ups are rapid; to avoid disincentives to private saving; to support strong financial supervision; to ensure strong corporate governance and efficient bankruptcy procedures; and to increase transparency across the spectrum of economic activities. Directors also encouraged authorities to enact policies that will enable early euro adoption—the growth-enhancing and vulnerability-

reducing opportunity unique to the CEECs. They considered that the adoption of the euro by the new EU member states should be predicated on a sound macroeconomic basis. This was seen as important especially to allow these countries sufficient flexibility to respond to asymmetric economic shocks in the absence of an independent monetary policy.

Directors considered that assessing the vulnerabilities associated with rapid catch-up—especially those related to strong capital inflows—will be the key challenge for Fund surveillance in the CEECs in the foreseeable future. Fund surveillance, Directors stressed, should encourage policies that are supportive of convergence, while closely monitoring accompanying vulnerabilities and helping to keep them contained. In this regard, several Directors noted that surveillance should focus on core issues related to macroeconomic and financial stability and its institutional underpinnings, while broad institutional development should remain the domain of development banks. Further, it was noted that Fund advice should continue to be sensitive to country-specific factors, while being mindful of the risk of potential adverse regional spillovers.

Recent Occasional Papers of the International Monetary Fund

252. Growth in the Central and Eastern European Countries of the European Union, by Susan Schadler, Ashoka Mody, Abdul Abiad, and Daniel Leigh. 2006.

251. The Design and Implementation of Deposit Insurance Systems, by David S. Hoelscher, Michael Taylor, and Ulrich H. Klueh. 2006.

250. Designing Monetary and Fiscal Policy in Low-Income Countries, by Abebe Aemro Selassie, Benedict Clements, Shamsuddin Tareq, Jan Kees Martijn, and Gabriel Di Bella. 2006.

249. Official Foreign Exchange Intervention, by Shogo Ishi, Jorge Iván Canales-Kriljenko, Roberto Guimarães, and Cem Karacadag. 2006.

248. Labor Market Performance in Transition: The Experience of Central and Eastern European Countries, by Jerald Schiff, Philippe Egoumé-Bossogo, Miho Ihara, Tetsuya Konuki, and Kornélia Krajnyák. 2006.

247. Rebuilding Fiscal Institutions in Post-Conflict Countries, by Sanjeev Gupta, Shamsuddin Tareq, Benedict Clements, Alex Segura-Ubiergo, Rina Bhattacharya, and Todd Mattina. 2005.

246. Experience with Large Fiscal Adjustments, by George C. Tsibouris, Mark A. Horton, Mark J. Flanagan, and Wojciech S. Maliszewski. 2005.

245. Budget System Reform in Emerging Economies: The Challenges and the Reform Agenda, by Jack Diamond. 2005.

244. Monetary Policy Implementation at Different Stages of Market Development, by a staff team led by Bernard J. Laurens. 2005.

243. Central America: Global Integration and Regional Cooperation, edited by Markus Rodlauer and Alfred Schipke. 2005.

242. Turkey at the Crossroads: From Crisis Resolution to EU Accession, by a staff team led by Reza Moghadam. 2005.

241. The Design of IMF-Supported Programs, by Atish Ghosh, Charis Christofides, Jun Kim, Laura Papi, Uma Ramakrishnan, Alun Thomas, and Juan Zalduendo. 2005.

240. Debt-Related Vulnerabilities and Financial Crises: An Application of the Balance Sheet Approach to Emerging Market Countries, by Christoph Rosenberg, Ioannis Halikias, Brett House, Christian Keller, Jens Nystedt, Alexander Pitt, and Brad Setser. 2005.

239. GEM: A New International Macroeconomic Model, by Tamim Bayoumi, with assistance from Douglas Laxton, Hamid Faruqee, Benjamin Hunt, Philippe Karam, Jaewoo Lee, Alessandro Rebucci, and Ivan Tchakarov. 2004.

238. Stabilization and Reforms in Latin America: A Macroeconomic Perspective on the Experience Since the Early 1990s, by Anoop Singh, Agnès Belaisch, Charles Collyns, Paula De Masi, Reva Krieger, Guy Meredith, and Robert Rennhack. 2005.

237. Sovereign Debt Structure for Crisis Prevention, by Eduardo Borensztein, Marcos Chamon, Olivier Jeanne, Paolo Mauro, and Jeromin Zettelmeyer. 2004.

236. Lessons from the Crisis in Argentina, by Christina Daseking, Atish R. Ghosh, Alun Thomas, and Timothy Lane. 2004.

235. A New Look at Exchange Rate Volatility and Trade Flows, by Peter B. Clark, Natalia Tamirisa, and Shang-Jin Wei, with Azim Sadikov and Li Zeng. 2004.

234. Adopting the Euro in Central Europe: Challenges of the Next Step in European Integration, by Susan M. Schadler, Paulo F. Drummond, Louis Kuijs, Zuzana Murgasova, and Rachel N. van Elkan. 2004.

233. Germany's Three-Pillar Banking System: Cross-Country Perspectives in Europe, by Allan Brunner, Jörg Decressin, Daniel Hardy, and Beata Kudela. 2004.

232. China's Growth and Integration into the World Economy: Prospects and Challenges, edited by Eswar Prasad. 2004.

231. Chile: Policies and Institutions Underpinning Stability and Growth, by Eliot Kalter, Steven Phillips, Marco A. Espinosa-Vega, Rodolfo Luzio, Mauricio Villafuerte, and Manmohan Singh. 2004.

230. Financial Stability in Dollarized Countries, by Anne-Marie Gulde, David Hoelscher, Alain Ize, David Marston, and Gianni De Nicoló. 2004.

229. Evolution and Performance of Exchange Rate Regimes, by Kenneth S. Rogoff, Aasim M. Husain, Ashoka Mody, Robin Brooks, and Nienke Oomes. 2004.

228. Capital Markets and Financial Intermediation in The Baltics, by Alfred Schipke, Christian Beddies, Susan M. George, and Niamh Sheridan. 2004.

227. U.S. Fiscal Policies and Priorities for Long-Run Sustainability, edited by Martin Mühleisen and Christopher Towe. 2004.

226. Hong Kong SAR: Meeting the Challenges of Integration with the Mainland, edited by Eswar Prasad, with contributions from Jorge Chan-Lau, Dora Iakova, William Lee, Hong Liang, Ida Liu, Papa N'Diaye, and Tao Wang. 2004.

225. Rules-Based Fiscal Policy in France, Germany, Italy, and Spain, by Teresa Dában, Enrica Detragiache, Gabriel di Bella, Gian Maria Milesi-Ferretti, and Steven Symansky. 2003.

224. Managing Systemic Banking Crises, by a staff team led by David S. Hoelscher and Marc Quintyn. 2003.

223. Monetary Union Among Member Countries of the Gulf Cooperation Council, by a staff team led by Ugo Fasano. 2003.

222. Informal Funds Transfer Systems: An Analysis of the Informal Hawala System, by Mohammed El Qorchi, Samuel Munzele Maimbo, and John F. Wilson. 2003.

221. Deflation: Determinants, Risks, and Policy Options, by Manmohan S. Kumar. 2003.

220. Effects of Financial Globalization on Developing Countries: Some Empirical Evidence, by Eswar S. Prasad, Kenneth Rogoff, Shang-Jin Wei, and Ayhan Kose. 2003.

219. Economic Policy in a Highly Dollarized Economy: The Case of Cambodia, by Mario de Zamaroczy and Sopanha Sa. 2003.

218. Fiscal Vulnerability and Financial Crises in Emerging Market Economies, by Richard Hemming, Michael Kell, and Axel Schimmelpfennig. 2003.

217. Managing Financial Crises: Recent Experience and Lessons for Latin America, edited by Charles Collyns and G. Russell Kincaid. 2003.

216. Is the PRGF Living Up to Expectations? An Assessment of Program Design, by Sanjeev Gupta, Mark Plant, Benedict Clements, Thomas Dorsey, Emanuele Baldacci, Gabriela Inchauste, Shamsuddin Tareq, and Nita Thacker. 2002.

215. Improving Large Taxpayers' Compliance: A Review of Country Experience, by Katherine Baer. 2002.

214. Advanced Country Experiences with Capital Account Liberalization, by Age Bakker and Bryan Chapple. 2002.

213. The Baltic Countries: Medium-Term Fiscal Issues Related to EU and NATO Accession, by Johannes Mueller, Christian Beddies, Robert Burgess, Vitali Kramarenko, and Joannes Mongardini. 2002.

212. Financial Soundness Indicators: Analytical Aspects and Country Practices, by V. Sundararajan, Charles Enoch, Armida San José, Paul Hilbers, Russell Krueger, Marina Moretti, and Graham Slack. 2002.

211. Capital Account Liberalization and Financial Sector Stability, by a staff team led by Shogo Ishii and Karl Habermeier. 2002.

210. IMF-Supported Programs in Capital Account Crises, by Atish Ghosh, Timothy Lane, Marianne Schulze-Ghattas, Aleš Bulíř, Javier Hamann, and Alex Mourmouras. 2002.

209. Methodology for Current Account and Exchange Rate Assessments, by Peter Isard, Hamid Faruqee, G. Russell Kincaid, and Martin Fetherston. 2001.

208. Yemen in the 1990s: From Unification to Economic Reform, by Klaus Enders, Sherwyn Williams, Nada Choueiri, Yuri Sobolev, and Jan Walliser. 2001.

207. Malaysia: From Crisis to Recovery, by Kanitta Meesook, Il Houng Lee, Olin Liu, Yougesh Khatri, Natalia Tamirisa, Michael Moore, and Mark H. Krysl. 2001.

206. The Dominican Republic: Stabilization, Structural Reform, and Economic Growth, by a staff team led by Philip Young comprising Alessandro Giustiniani, Werner C. Keller, and Randa E. Sab and others. 2001.

205. Stabilization and Savings Funds for Nonrenewable Resources, by Jeffrey Davis, Rolando Ossowski, James Daniel, and Steven Barnett. 2001.

Note: For information on the titles and availability of Occasional Papers not listed, please consult the IMF's *Publications Catalog* or contact IMF Publication Services.